Nameless, Blameless, and Without Shame

INTERFACES

Series Editor: Barbara Green, O.P.

# Nameless, Blameless, and Without Shame

Two Cannibal Mothers Before a King

*Gina Hens-Piazza*

A Michael Glazier Book

**LITURGICAL PRESS**

Collegeville, Minnesota

www.litpress.org

A Michael Glazier Book published by the Liturgical Press

Cover design by Ann Blattner. Watercolor by Ethel Boyle.

1    2    3    4    5    6    7    8

**Library of Congress Cataloging-in-Publication Data**

Hens-Piazza, Gina, 1948–
    Nameless, blameless, and without shame : two cannibal mothers before a king / Gina Hens-Piazza.
        p.  cm. — (Interfaces (Collegeville, Minn.))
    "A Michael Glazier book."
    Includes bibliographical references.
    ISBN 0-8146-5961-6 (alk. paper)
        1. Bible. O.T. Kings, 2nd, VI, 24–33—Criticism, interpretation, etc.
    2. Characters and characteristics in the Bible. 3. Cannibalism in the Bible.
    I. Title.  II. Interfaces (Collegeville, Minn.)
    BS1335.6.C36 H46 2003
    222'.5406—dc21                                                          2002035250

# For my Mother
on her eightieth birthday

*"For in life with her, there is no pain, gladness only and joy."*
(Wis 8:16)

# CONTENTS

# PREFACE

The book you hold in your hand is one of six volumes in a new set. This series, called INTERFACES, is a curriculum and scholarly adventure, a creative opportunity in teaching and learning, presented at this moment in the long story of how the Bible has been studied, interpreted, and appropriated.

The INTERFACES project was prompted by a number of experiences that you, perhaps, share. When I first taught undergraduates the college had just received a substantial grant from the National Endowment for the Humanities, and one of the recurring courses designed within the grant was called Great Figures in Pursuit of Excellence. Three courses would be taught, each centering on a figure from some academic discipline or other, with a common seminar section to provide occasion for some integration. Some triads were more successful than others, as you might imagine. But the opportunity to concentrate on a single individual—whether historical or literary—to team teach, to make links to another pair of figures, and to learn new things about other disciplines was stimulating and fun for all involved. A second experience that gave rise to the present series came at the same time, connected also with undergraduates. It was my frequent experience to have Roman Catholic students feel quite put out about taking "more" biblical studies since, as they confidently affirmed, they had already been there many times and done it all. That was, of course, not true; as we well know, there is always more to learn. And often those who felt most informed were the least likely to take on new information when offered it.

A stimulus as primary as my experience with students was the familiarity of listening to friends and colleagues at professional meetings talking about the research that excites us most. I often wondered: Do her undergraduate students know about this? Or how does he bring these ideas—clearly so energizing to him—into the college classroom? Perhaps some of us have felt bored with classes that seem wholly unrelated to research, that rehash the same familiar material repeatedly. Hence the idea for this series of books to bring to the fore and combine some of our research interest with our teaching and learning. Accordingly, this series is not so much about creating texts *for* student audiences, but rather about *sharing* our scholarly passions with them. Because these volumes are intended each as a piece of original scholarship they are geared to be stimulating to both students and established scholars, perhaps resulting in some fruitful collaborative learning adventures.

The series also developed from a widely-shared sense that all academic fields are expanding and exploding, and that to contemplate "covering" even a testament (let alone the whole Bible or Western monotheistic religions) needs to be abandoned in favor of something with greater depth. At the same time the links between our fields are becoming increasingly obvious as well, and we glimpse exciting possibilities for ways of working that will draw together academic realms that once seemed separate. Finally, the spark of enthusiasm that almost always ignites when I mention to colleagues and students the idea of single figures in combination—interfacing—encourages me that this is an idea worth trying.

And so with the leadership and help of Liturgical Press Academic Editor Linda Maloney, as well as with the encouragement and support of Managing Editor Mark Twomey, the series has begun to take shape.

Each volume in the INTERFACES series focuses clearly on a biblical character (or perhaps a pair of them). The characters are in some cases powerful (King Saul, Pontius Pilate) and familiar (John the Baptist, Joseph) though in other cases they will strike many as minor and little-known (the Cannibal Mothers, Herodias). In any case, each of them has been chosen to open up a set of worlds for consideration. The named (or unnamed) character interfaces with his or her historical-cultural world and its many issues, with other characters from biblical literature; each character has drawn forth the creativity of the author, who has taken on the challenge of engaging many readers. The books are specifically designed for college students (though we think suitable for some graduate work as well), planned to provide young adults with relevant information and at a level of critical sophistication that matches the rest of the undergraduate curriculum. In fact, the expectation is that what students are learning in other classes on historiography, literary theory, and cultural anthropology will find an echo in these books, each of which is explicit about at least two relevant methodologies. It is surely the case that biblical studies is in a methodology-conscious moment, and the INTERFACES series embraces it enthusiastically. Our hope is for students (and teachers) to continue to see the relationship between their best questions and their most valuable insights, between how they approach texts and what they find there. The volumes go well beyond familiar paraphrase of narratives to ask questions that are relevant in our era. At the same time the series authors have each dealt with the notion of the Bible as Scripture in a way that is comfortable for them. None of the books is preachy or hortatory, and yet the self-implicating aspects of working with the revelatory text are handled frankly. The assumption is, again, that college can be a good time for students to rethink their beliefs and assumptions, and they need to do so in good company.

The INTERFACES volumes are not substitutes for the Bible. In every case they are to be read with the text. Quoting has been kept to a minimum for that very reason. The volumes, when used in a classroom setting, are accompanied by a companion volume, *From Earth's Creation to John's Revelation: The INTERFACES Biblical Storyline Companion,* which provides a quick, straightforward overview of the whole storyline into which the characters under special study fit. Web links will also be available through the Liturgical Press website: www.litpress.org.

The series challenge—for publisher, writers, teachers, and students—is to combine the volumes creatively, to "interface" them well so that the vast potential of the biblical text continues to unfold for all of us. The first six volumes: in Old Testament/Hebrew Bible featuring Saul, the Cannibal Mothers, and Joseph; in New Testament focusing on John the Baptist, Herodias, and Pontius Pilate, offer a foretaste of other volumes currently in preparation. It has been a pleasure, and a richly informative privilege, to work with the authors of these first volumes as well as the series consultants: Carleen Mandolfo for Hebrew Bible and Catherine Murphy for New Testament. It is the hope of all of us that you will find the series useful and stimulating for your own teaching and learning.

Barbara Green, O.P.
INTERFACES Series Editor
June 29, 2002
Berkeley, California

# ACKNOWLEDGMENTS

I am so fortunate to have wonderful colleagues here at the Jesuit School of Theology and at the Graduate Theological Union in Berkeley. Their willingness to devote faculty colloquiums to this work as well as their individual comments, questions, and criticisms have consistently supported me in this endeavor. I am also privileged to have such talented and probing students. Their persistent questions on matters of the hostility and violence surrounding stories of biblical women have prompted my work here. I am especially grateful for those who have not only been willing to think with me on these matters but who have heard versions of these chapters delivered as lectures at various stages in their composition.

Others have also contributed in various ways during this work. I am grateful for my colleagues in the Hermeneutics Task Force of the Catholic Biblical Association. Their willingness to read and discuss some of this material during its earliest stages has been an enormous help. Barbara Green, editor of the Interfaces Series, has been a steady source of encouragement as well as a cherished friend. Without her vision of this series, an extended study of these two biblical women might have never materialized.

To three people in particular I owe an enormous debt. Bula Maddison's relentless close reading and corrections helped to bring good order to each and every paragraph. Ann Naffziger's exquisite attention to copyediting rendered the final polish for a finished product. Hannah Hens-Piazza, my daughter, came to my assistance when, in the final weeks of a finished manuscript, the wonders of technology failed me and demonstrated some of a computer's most drastic shortcomings. The steadfastness and generosity of each of these women evokes my deepest admiration and respect. Each of them is in her own way an inspiration to me. My gratitude to them is heartfelt and immense.

PART I

# CHAPTER ONE

## *Building Character*

When I was growing up I used to complain a lot about having to do household chores. In my rebellious adolescence I deemed such menial tasks as cleaning my bedroom, washing windows, or sweeping floors "tedious," "repetitive," or "boring." My mother, determined to short-circuit my outcry, would match my objections by pointing out an inherent reward for doing such work. Bent upon securing my cooperation, she would coax my compliance with her rapid-fire rebuttals. "This kind of work builds character," she would say. And though I was never quite convinced of such benefits, her tone of voice convinced me that it was time to end the impasse and get to work.

This study is also about building character. However, the task before us is not menial—nor is it repetitive, tedious, or boring. Actually it is a kind of work that we often do quite unconsciously. When it is intentional, character building can be engaging, creative, and thus satisfying labor. This is a task where readers build characters in texts, and in the process character is being built in the readers. It is a reciprocal task; each process serves the other. The potential for such exchanges always exists when readers and literature meet. However, the prospects for character building between texts and readers is especially abundant and pronounced in the biblical texts. Granted, this may seem odd, because we tend to think of the Bible as a religious text. But the Bible is also a rich literary treasure boasting some of the most familiar story lines, aesthetic accomplishments, and captivating characters within the halls of literature. There is hardly a college textbook introducing the study of literature that does not register some of the biblical stories among its selections.

During the past fifty years biblical studies has trained its attention on this immense literary richness. Though profoundly important as religious texts, the biblical writings are also recognized as ranking among the world's greatest literary achievements. Unfolding across these texts, exquisite literary artistry transmits a depth of theological inquiry. Like other noteworthy literary classics, the Bible is an immense cache of stylistic devices and poetic features. Working together, these craft a compendium of cherished faith statements. Even a cursory glance across the biblical canon reveals a vast mosaic of literary genius. Poems, novellas, songs, legends, speeches, etc. artfully manifest a people's religious convictions about their God. Hence the profundity of religious content here is skillfully matched and complemented by a profundity of literary form.

In conjunction with the Bible's reputation as literary pinnacle these writings have produced some of the most compelling and familiar characters in the world of literature. Names such as Moses, Esther, David, and Bathsheba reference a few of the towering personages we associate with the Bible's literary store. So enduring and compelling are the characters of these influential figures that they have not remained confined to the pages of the Bible. The immensity and complexity of these figures often burst forth from the covers of the sacred texts to become the frequent subjects of painting, sculpture, film, novels, and other kinds of representative art. From Cecil B. DeMille's 1960 film *The Ten Commandments* to the recent Disney animated movie *Prince of Egypt,* Moses' character has made frequent appearances beyond the pages of the Bible. David too has a life beyond the biblical confines. Visitors to Florence do not quickly forget Michelangelo's towering statue of this famous king of Israel. Such preoccupation with these individuals suggests the gripping and compelling nature of the characters in this text. How is it that the Bible has been able to produce such alluring and influential characters? Or to put it another way, by what means does character building—or to use the literary term, "characterization"—take place in these texts?

## The Role of Texts in Character Building

For a long time literary theory defined characters as the sum of the words used to describe them. Characters were equal to the words in the text about them and the words in the text spoken by them. Characters about whom most was written, or who had the most to say in a story, or whose actions navigated the course of the whole narrative were the primary focus of investigation. They were dubbed "main characters," "round characters," or "major characters." Their characterhood was always evaluated as the center of the plot controlling the direction of the storyline. Characters about whom less information was provided or about whom little reference was made were considered "minor characters." Often they were nameless and made only a momentary appearance in a tale. In some circles they have also been designated as "flat characters" or "agents" whose sole function was in the service of advancing the plot or highlighting the main characters.

In Exod 2:16-22 Moses has fled from Egypt after killing an Egyptian. The Pharaoh's determination to kill him for his murderous deed had prompted Moses' rapid exit. Now settled safely in Midian, Moses rests at a well where the daughters of a local priest of the region have come to water their father's flocks. When some shepherds drive the women away Moses rises up and comes to their rescue. Afterward he waters the flocks for them, accepts their father's invitation of hospitality, and marries one of the Midianite's daughters, Zipporah.

According to the literary specifications discussed above, Moses gets the designation "major character." Most of the narrative is explicitly about him. While the conflict involves the daughters of the priest of Midian, Moses' action brings about the resolution of the conflict and thus sets the direction of the plot. By contrast, the daughters are "minor characters." Nameless, they seem to be in the narrative primarily to introduce crisis. Moreover, the crisis appears to be in the service of highlighting the centrality of Moses and magnifying his virtuous deeds. He has more to say than the daughters. The narrator says more about him than any other character. Hence both characterization and the designation "major" or "minor" stem largely from a kind of quantitative assessment. Most of the narrative is directly or indirectly focused on Moses. This is his story.

Such kinds of character evaluations are typical and are often charted according to four dimensions of description found in the text: (1) the descriptions of physical features or appearance, (2) the portrayal of a character's inner life, (3) the words spoken by the character, and (4) the actions of the individual.[1] While our discussion of character building will not be limited solely to what the text says about an individual in the story, these four features do come into play. Thus we will rehearse them here.

First there are those descriptions sketching a character's exterior appearance and identity. These are often provided by the narrator when a character is introduced. The opening chapters of the book of Esther present

---

[1] For a more extended discussion along these four lines see Adele Berlin, *Poetics and Interpretation of Biblical Narrative* (Winona Lake: Eisenbrauns, 1994); Robert Alter, *The Art of Biblical Narrative* (New York: Basic Books, 1981); Meir Sternberg, *The Poetics of Biblical Narrative: Ideological Literature and the Drama of Reading* (Bloomington: Indiana University Press, 1989); Shimon Bar Efrat, *Narrative Art in the Bible* (Sheffield: Almond Press, 1989).

the soon-to-be-queen as "a girl, fair and beautiful" (Esth 2:7).[2] Though each subsequent reference to Esther's appearance (i. e., 2:9, 15-18; 15:1-5; 5:1; 9:29-32) provides little information in itself, gradually an image of her accumulates across the narrative. After "fair and beautiful" in 2:7 we learn that this orphan girl was adopted by the king and in 2:9 provided with cosmetics and maids; in 2:15 she is "admired by all who saw her"; by 5:1 she has put on "royal robes" and is standing "in the inner court of the king's palace." Hence by the end of the story the portrait emerges of a bold and mature queen who has the courage to save her people. The "girl, fair and beautiful" at the beginning of the story is now a woman who possesses a beauty that is far more than skin deep.

In another instance David is about to become the focus of the long story of Israel's monarchy beginning in 1 Samuel. The storyteller introduces him as "a ruddy youth, of comely appearance" (1 Sam 6:12). Description of his physical appearance multiplies across the narrative as David grows to be a man, a military leader, and a king. Finally, in 1 Kings 1:1 David is on his deathbed. In keeping with his problematic relation to power over the years of his reign and its diminishing effect on his character he is now described in the least glorious of terms. He is "unable to get warm" although they "covered him with clothes." David's character comes full circle. From his rise to the heights of kingship to his decline on his deathbed where he is old and cold, we see the complex development of his character over a lifetime.

Often the physical description of the biblical character is quite general. This is true of three characters, Absalom, Abishag, and Bathsheba, who appear in the course of the story of David's kingship. Absalom is David's son. Abishag is a young woman brought to David when he is old. Bathsheba is one of David's wives. Though appearing in different stories, Absalom, Abishag, and Bathsheba are each described in very general terms as "beautiful." However, in the course of each of their stories such a vague characterization as "beautiful" is variously elaborated by intermittent attention to detail. For example, we hear about Absalom's hair: "When he cut the hair of his head—and he would cut it every year; he would cut it then because it grew too heavy for him—he would weigh the hair; two hundred shekels, king's weight" (2 Sam 14:25-26). Or we hear that Abishag is a young virgin (1 Kings 1:3-4) from Shunem and that she "looked after the king and waited on him." A character's clothing, facial features, physical stature, age, parentage, social role, equipment, hair, etc. number among the frequently cited visible attributes that give the physical description greater definition

---

[2] All biblical quotations are taken from the *NRSV* unless otherwise noted.

and detail. In one of the most extreme examples (1 Sam 17:5-7) we are not only offered a description of Goliath as gigantic but must endure a detailed account of his military paraphernalia. He wears

> a helmet of bronze on his head, and he was armed with a coat of mail; the weight of the coat was five thousand shekels of bronze. He had greaves of bronze on his legs and a javelin of bronze slung between his shoulders.

The detail here not only affords description of this Philistine giant. The elaboration of the metal attire attesting to the great weight of the armor provides evidence of his gigantic size.

By contrast, in 2 Sam 6:14 we encounter David, dancing before the ark in a state of relative undress. In this instance the description attends not so much to what he wears but to his lack of clothing. "And David danced whirling around before YHWH with all his might, wearing only a linen loincloth around him." This passing mention of brief attire later becomes a point of controversy that will lead to further character development when his wife Michal comes out to meet him. Across these narratives we encounter numerous instances of physical features being highlighted. Leah's eyes (Gen 29:17), Tamar's clothing (2 Sam 13:18-19), Meribbaal's lameness (2 Sam 4:4), Samson's hair (Judg 16:13-17)—these and other similar details shape our first impressions in the process of character building.

More often than not these physical descriptions serve to develop not only the character but also the story line. For example, in the story of Isaac and his twin sons, Jacob and Esau, the plot development is tied to the description of these characters. Isaac is "blind" and Jacob and Esau are described as "smooth skin" and "hairy one" respectively. In order for Jacob to trick his sightless father into granting him his father's blessing, intended for his older brother Esau, he must disguise himself. Hence the physical description of Jacob as "smooth skin" is not just an interesting detail about his appearance; rather, it serves as explanation of why Jacob's ruse before his blind father Isaac warranted his animal-skin disguise (Gen 27:15-16).

I spoke of four dimensions of description, of which the first was physical appearance. Second on the list is how references to a character's inner life also come into play. Such disclosures make readers privy to characters' thoughts, motives, feelings, inward conversations, spiritual and personal struggles. It may be the storyteller, i.e., the person we call the narrator, who relates the character's interiority or it may be the characters themselves. For instance, the narrative reveals that Saul, the first king of Israel, is continually overshadowed in popularity by the young warrior

David. As the story unfolds we hear that "Saul was very angry" and he "turned a jealous eye on David from that day forward" (1 Sam 18:6-9). In another story Abraham is told that despite their old age he and his wife Sarah will conceive a child. Sarah, who is in earshot inside the tent, "laughs inside herself" when she hears the pronouncement (Gen 18:12). Such inner feelings can also be expressed indirectly. For example, Elijah, the prophet in Israel, has escaped to the wilderness in order to evade the death sentence that Jezebel has pronounced concerning him. Alone in the wilderness, Elijah expresses a wish to die: "Oh LORD, I have had enough, take my life," implying a demeanor of despondency (1 Kings 19:4). In another instance David's son Absalom has killed his brother and been exiled from the country as a result. That the narrative tells us David's heart is fixed on his exiled son Absalom (2 Sam 13:39) suggests the complexity of feelings David as both king and father harbors as a consequence of these events. Again and again words work both directly and indirectly to craft the inner lives of characters and to provide the reader with access to this private realm.

Third, characters are also crafted indirectly by what they say. A character's own words can suggest something about his or her personality as well as fashion impressions about his or her relationships with others. For example, Moses' words show how reluctantly he takes on the life work God assigns to him: "Who am I that I should go to Pharaoh and bring the children of Israel out of Egypt?" (Exod 3:11). We hear King Solomon's absolute power speak when he orders his officer, Benaiah, to kill Joab, a suspected insurrectionist who is clinging to the corner of the altar for protection: "Strike him down and bury him" (1 Kings 2:31). Given the convention that a person clinging to the horns of the altar is immune from harm, Solomon's words suggest his own sense of his unqualified power as king. He believes he has the right to bypass even religious protocol.

Fourth and last in our list, characters' actions also tell us about them—and at times their actions speak louder than their words. Their deeds craft a mental image of the character that animates them. In the biblical story of Jacob and Esau we are given an early glimpse of Jacob's craftiness when he demands the birthright of his starving brother Esau in exchange for a little soup (Gen 25:29-34). Later, another story catalogues the actions that both he and his mother, Rebekah, execute in order to steal his father Isaac's blessing, intended for Esau.

> So he *went* and *got* them [kid goats] and *brought* them to his mother; and his mother *prepared* savory food, such as his father loved. Then Rebekah *took* the best garments of her elder son Esau, which were with her in the house, and *put* them on her younger son Jacob; and she

*put* the skins of the kids on his hands and on the smooth part of his neck. Then she *handed* the savory food, and the bread that she had *prepared,* to her son Jacob. So he *went* in to his father, and *said,* "My father." (Gen 27:14-17)

This litany of actions contributes to the portrait of Jacob as unhappily shrewd and even reprehensible. Similarly, in another story Elijah, the prophet in Israel, is trying to win the hearts of the people back to YHWH. In one short event nine different verbs work to describe Elijah's actions and speech on Mt. Carmel.

Then Elijah *said* to all the people, "Come closer to me"; and all the people came closer to him. First he *repaired* the altar of the LORD that had been thrown down; Elijah *took* twelve stones, according to the number of the tribes of the sons of Jacob, to whom the word of the LORD came, *saying,* "Israel shall be your name": with the stones he *built* an altar in the name of the LORD. Then he *made* a trench around the altar, large enough to contain two measures of seed. Next he *put* the wood in order, *cut* the bull in pieces, and *laid* it on the wood. He *said,* "Fill four jars with water and pour it on the burnt offering and on the wood." Then he *said,* "Do it a second time"; and they did it a second time. Again he *said,* "Do it a third time"; and they did it a third time, so that the water ran all around the altar, and filled the trench also with water.

At the time of the offering of the oblation the prophet Elijah *came* near and said, "O LORD, God of Abraham, Isaac, and Israel, let it be known this day that you are God in Israel, that I am your servant, and that I have done all these things at your bidding. Answer me, O LORD, answer me, so that this people may know that you, O LORD, are God, and that you have turned their hearts back." (1 Kings 18:30-37)

This parade of verbs not only works to get the people's attention but also adds to our impression of the determination of this prophet's character. Actions and words combine to provide a vivid and animated portrait of the prophet bent on converting the wayward hearts of the people. Thus we observe that when such features as actions and words are tallied alongside physical descriptions and references to the prophet's inner life a character begins to emerge out of the words of the text. "*Begins*" might be the key word here. As we shall see, character building involves much more than these four textual features just described. Is our image of Elijah or of any biblical character confined only to what the words of the story convey? Are characters merely the sum total of words contained in the texts—those spoken about them and those spoken by them? Or are these words only the locus where character building *begins*?

## The Role of Readers in Character Building

Robert Alter notes a real curiosity about biblical characters that challenges the notion of characters being equal to the sum of the words in a text.[3] He observes that while interpretations and representations outside the Bible tend to portray characters such as Moses, Esther, David, or Bathsheba with depth and complexity they are in fact, by most literary standards, "thinly" drawn in their biblical story world. When compared to the sharply detailed portraits of personalities we encounter in Western literature or, for that matter, placed alongside the heroes of the great Greek classics, the biblical characters appear rudimentary. Biblical characters say less, do less, and are described in relatively more general terms as compared to their Western or Greek counterparts. Sparsely sketched in the text, their depiction might be labeled "minimalist" at best. For example, when King David is strolling on his roof one evening he sees a woman named Bathsheba bathing, and he commands his officers to go and bring her to him. A description of Bathsheba as "beautiful" does not really give much information or create a very defined image of what David saw when he looked out at her from his roof porch (2 Sam 11:2). Yet, prompted by that text, countless interpreters and artists seem to have gotten a substantial impression of just what David saw. Bathsheba has been the subject of numerous and elaborate representations founded on David's voyeurism and that of subsequent generations of readers.[4]

In another example David, the new king in Israel, is bringing the Ark of the Covenant into the capital city Jerusalem. The sacredness with which the ark was regarded warranted that great fear, awe, and care be expended in transporting it. As the Ark enters the city, David, scantily dressed, is leading the way with an ecstatic dance seen by all those who assembled as well as by his wife Michal. She is described as "watching from the window and she saw King David leaping and dancing before the LORD" (2 Sam 6:16). On this brief description numerous depictions of Michal have been founded. Etched in stone, portrayed in movies, and painted on canvas, the image of the woman in the window has received widespread notoriety and attention.[5]

---

[3] Alter, *The Art of Biblical Narrative* 56.

[4] See J. Cheryl Exum, *Plotted, Shot, and Painted: Cultural Representations of Biblical Women* (Sheffield: Sheffield Academic Press, 1996) 19–53.

[5] Ibid. 54–79.

Given their abbreviated descriptions, how is it that biblical characters such as Bathsheba and Michal are endowed with such rich and complex characterhoods in the tradition of interpretation or even in the history of artistic representations? Why are they so recognizable, so vivid, so indelible? How is it that they are so well known? Contemporary literary theory argues that characters don't live completely and exclusively in a text. They are much more than what the text supplies about them. Their textual imprint is only an initial draft. The reader also plays a significant role in fashioning the players in stories.[6] And this is true not just of biblical characters but of all the heroes and villains, protagonists and antagonists, major characters and minor characters across a literature's vast landscape. Moreover, the less said about a character, the more our imagination must supply the coloring and definitive lines in the process of painting the portrait.

In the case of biblical characters that are so sparsely drawn in the text, readers must play an especially pronounced role. While the text provides an initial version of David, Moses, or Esther, we subsequently supply draft upon draft each time we encounter these individuals in their story world. Such characters are, at first, the outcome of the words in the text, but their development doesn't stop there. They are also further fashioned, elaborated, and even reconstructed during the reading process. They are not limited to the quantity of words on a page. When characters drawn on the page encounter a reader they eclipse the meager biblical depiction and undergo vast and elaborate redrawing. As we get to know them or as we try to "figure them out" we read between the lines. We predict their actions, anticipate their responses, or imagine the feelings they might have. We begin to have expectations of them or construct notions of what they must be like interpersonally. We form impressions based not only on what we know but also on what we can surmise or infer from the textural evidence. What we don't know we often provide, until we come upon other information in a story that confirms or contradicts what we have constructed.

Soon a character such as Bathsheba is more than just that text's vague description "beautiful" (2 Sam 11:2). Bathsheba is looked at during her bath in her own court. However, there is nothing in the text to indicate that she invited this viewing. In fact, given the privacy of a woman's act of bathing, there is much to suggest that David's act would have been an intrusion against her will. Next, Bathsheba is sent for and slept with by this king. The first and only time we hear Bathsheba say anything in this story, she sends

---

[6] The work of Seymour Chatman, *Story and Discourse* (Ithaca: Cornell University Press, 1978) and Baruch Hochman, *Character in Literature* (Ithaca: Cornell University Press, 1985) have been particularly influential in reformulating contemporary character theory.

word to the king: "I am with child" (11:5) as a result of these events. As we consider what the culture of monarchy was like we begin to feel the weight of the subjugation experienced by citizens ruled by a monarch. Hence we can easily imagine the fear that occasioned Bathsheba's inability to say no, or to say anything, to a king's order.

As we read between the lines of the story we might relate Bathsheba to other oppressed women we know or read about. Thus we begin to empathize with her as a woman violated. But our empathy for her doesn't stop there. When David hears that she bears within her the evidence of his misdeed he schemes a coverup. He sends for Uriah, Bathsheba's husband who is away at a battle dutifully fulfilling his military obligation. The king anticipates that Uriah will return home to his house and immediately sleep with his wife. However, David's ploy to pass off evidence of his paternity fails when Uriah refuses to stay in his own home while his countrymen are fighting. The sadness we might assign Bathsheba multiplies when we learn to what lengths this king will go to cover his adulterous tracks. Desperate but determined, David orders that Uriah be put in the front line of battle and killed. Not only has this woman been violated and impregnated by this ruler, she has also lost her husband. Hence the abbreviated and general depiction of Bathsheba in the text as "beautiful" is now extended and elaborated by a complex and conflicted interiority. With our own contemporary awareness of violence and its victims we recognize patterns between what we know from our experience and what we read in the text. Gradually we infuse an emotional life of suffering and affliction into this otherwise thinly drawn character described only as "beautiful."

Baruch Hochman refers to this process of character building as "reading out" characters from their context.[7] Ironic, this "reading out" occurs as we "read in" to the text. We shape a character out of our experience, out of what is familiar, out of what rings true, and out of an amplitude of associations we bring to the tale. This idea suggests that the very nature of the character is open-ended, subject to numerous fashionings and refashionings. The character is the vision of our speculation, constructed each time we come to a story. However, a character is not anything we make him or her to be. This is not an arbitrary projection of ourselves into the story, nor is it an extension of some unbridled fantasies rendering characters fit for the cover of tabloids. Our speculations and constructions cannot overrun the story. The text sets limits to our construction. The words of the text serve as the clay out of which we sculpt the character. While the experience we bring to

---

[7] Hochman, *Character in Literature* 39.

the text will have a great deal to do with what we discover there, the characters we encounter must begin with and be grounded in the text.

## Building Our Character

Texts provide the initial descriptions that are our starting points. They also give other data that can be clarified or elaborated with outside research so as to contribute more information about a character. Within these boundaries we can draw analogies between our lives and the lives of characters. We make connections between patterns of behavior, modes of being, foibles and shortcomings, strengths and aptitudes, putting our lives alongside those we see in the text. We recognize and elaborate potential vices or virtues in characters because we are aware of those same well-developed vices and virtues in ourselves or in others in our experience. We latch onto hints of the familiar in characters, rounding out what the text provides with what we know from our own limited horizons or from the wider horizons of others whom we've read about. Hence the character is not only the product of what the text says, but grows, develops, and keeps on "becoming" with each new reader and each rereading.

This process of character building is not confined to the characters we encounter in texts. As we shape and imbue those characters with depth and dimension, character is being built in ourselves as readers. We may find characters whose strengths and their growing edges we identify with. At times they give us a glance at dimensions of ourselves that might otherwise go unseen. They can act as mirrors whose reflections help us to better see and understand ourselves.

Characters may inspire us. They may provide a helpful image we cling to in the face of adversity. They may be valued mentors at times when we need confidence. At other times the very image of a character we read in and out of a text may serve to challenge us. It may nudge us beyond cherished fears or complacencies. It may serve as a daily reminder of what we want to be.

Characters can also repel us. They can be our enemy. But because we construct them ourselves we are less apt to fear them. We can learn to face them, confront them, be vulnerable before them, or even gain insight about ourselves or others in real life and the way they constitute the opposition. Because characters are safe they have the capacity to prompt us to confront what is not safe or secure in our lives or in our relationships. They can serve as mantras that keep us on course or as icons that invite us to go deeper into self-understanding. Hence while character building is the effect of reading, it can also affect the reader. In the process of building characters in cooperation with the text, character is, at the same time, being built in us as readers.

Now, this whole enterprise of character building is really not so unfamiliar. It is a lot like meeting and getting to know people in our own lives. At first we might have some initial information about a person—we might see them at a distance or read about them or have access to hearsay about where they live, their family, their job. We might have some knowledge of what they are like. What others say about them and how others relate to them also informs what we think. This initial information might be piecemeal, minuscule, or extensive data. Then we encounter the person. How they look, what they say, and how they say it either advances or changes our first impression.

In this first encounter we might try to relate to what about them is similar to our own lives. Often we latch on to what is familiar about an individual. The person might look like someone we've known before or talk a lot like a friend from our past. We advance our understanding by relating the person's experiences to our own. But if we continue to build our acquaintance the mutuality of the relationship begins to reveal this person's uniqueness. Gradually his or her individuality emerges. As we behold all the features that make the person different from us we learn more about ourselves. In the same way, as we disclose more of ourselves to the other we often gain greater access to who they are. With each encounter we gain deeper understanding of this individual as well as deeper understanding about ourselves. For example, we might learn how hard someone has had to work at overcoming a learning disability in order to succeed in college. In turn this qualifies the stature and importance we assign to our own easy success at schoolwork and the credit we give ourselves.

Sometimes over the course of these disclosures we find that the person we first encountered is quite different than we expected. Persons we were initially attracted to, whom we really wanted to get to know, are not at all what we expected them to be. Conversely, the quiet person who is easily ignored or has little to say in a large social gathering turns out to be the most interesting. Over time our understanding of a person develops and changes. We might find an individual far more engaging or friendly than we first thought, or we might experience him or her as unexpectedly immature or superficial in the long run. In turn this affords us opportunities for learning about ourselves. We may ask ourselves questions: What is it that attracted us to them? Why did we want to get to know them? In the course of such musings we may discover that what others say about someone or the social status someone holds weighs too heavily in forming our opinions or in determining whom we seek out. Hence in the process of getting to know others we gain knowledge and insights about ourselves.

## Major and Minor Characters

As characterization theory shifts away from a focus riveted solely upon the text toward attention to the exchanges between text and reader, other shifts also occur. In earlier literary theory categories such as "major" and "minor" or "round" and "flat" drew distinctions between characters in a tale. We already noted that most often the characters about whom most was said or characters who had the most to say were considered to be the main or major characters. Characterization studies tended to focus on them because the text provided the most words and information about them. Thus major characters were of greatest interest, the ones we knew most about, the ones most important in the story, and thus the ones we tended to identify with. However, categories of "major" and "minor" were not exclusively a quantitative matter based on the number of words in the text. Storytellers also played a most influential part in evoking these designations. Earlier we called the storytellers "narrators." They are the voice that tells the story, introduces characters, announces the change of scenes, navigates the plot, and offers concluding summations. Grammatically they speak in the third person, telling the whole story as it unfolds. Their status as "emcee" gives us the impression that narrators are outsiders.

For a long time narrators and their status as storytellers have enjoyed an unearned confidence and credibility on the part of readers. Narrators have the authority to determine whose story is being told, who has the most to say, and who is silent. Their third-person narration determines who can speak and who can't. Narrators' third-person status gave the impression of an impartial authority in the story, a person whose perspective on persons and events could be trusted. In the past, characterization theory exempted narrators from our scrutiny. Narrators were protected from the suspicions and questions we put to characters. We allowed narrators to decide what characters we know most about and what characters we tend to ignore.

But narrators are not authors.[8] Narrators, like other players who make up the story, are part of the textual world. Though more elusive, they themselves are characters. Like others in the story they can be scrutinized based on their words. Whom they attend to and ally with, how they relate an event and what they choose *not* to relate can craft their image as a character. Hence, though narrators may indicate by means of their introduction

---

[8] Recent discussion of the role of the narrator reminds us of the narrator's role as a character and that we are always reading the narrator's version of the story. See Alice Bach, "Signs of the Flesh: Observations on Characterization in the Bible," *Semeia* 63 (1993) 61–79; John A. Darr, "Narrator as Character: Mapping a Reader-Oriented Approach to Narration in Luke-Acts," *Semeia* 63 (1993) 43–60.

and description whom they deem the major players in a story to be, readers might make other assessments. Take for example the text we considered earlier. In Exod 2:15b-22 the seven daughters of a priest of Midian are shepherding their fathers' flocks when some men come along and threaten them. Moses, who happens to be in the region, defends the women, waters their sheep, and ends up being taken in, fed, and provided a wife by the women's father, Reuel. The narrator tells the story in a way that focuses on Moses. The story opens with the narrator spotlighting him: "Moses fled from Pharaoh. He settled in the land of Midian and sat down by a well." It closes with the same attention on Moses. "Moses agreed to stay with the man and he gave Moses his daughter Zipporah in marriage." Throughout this brief tale the narrator tells this story as Moses' story. However, a reader might choose to resist the narrator's focus on Moses at Midian and instead focus on the priest's unnamed daughters. In another, longer story (1 Kings 1–11) the narrator rivets our attention on King Solomon and all his elaborate building projects. A reader could cooperate with the narrator and admire this powerful ruler and all his accomplishments, or that reader could decide to ignore the narrator's focus on Solomon. Instead she could direct her attention to all the nameless "laborers" mentioned in passing across these chapters who have been drafted into four months of annual service to complete this monarch's elaborate building projects.

In contemporary literary circles characterization studies accord less authority to the narrator in determining what characters to study. Instead, the reader as well as the text determine the character's eligibility for attention. While the character must be in the text, which character becomes the focus for attention is largely dependent on readers' interests and experiences, their own identities, and what they seek to learn. Consequently, categories such as major and minor become less appropriate as lenses through which to look at characters in a story. As the reader's role is taken into account, more is less and less is more in character building. The more information provided about a character, the less the readers need to involve themselves in character building. The less said about a character, the more the readers must become involved in filling the gaps. This creates greater investment and interest on the part of readers in some characters and a diminished interest and concern with others. Moreover, given readers' tendency to identify with a particular character or characters, a reader's own identity comes into play in determining who is of interest or importance in a tale. Hence attending to this engagement of text and readers in the business of character building is not only redefining how a character is developed but is also erasing some of the categories, such as major and minor, that have limited the attention to some characters and thus prevented their development. The following brief vignette will illustrate what we have been saying here.

\* \* \* \* \*

Let's suppose for a moment you were one of six college students to be honored for community service at an awards reception. When you arrived at the four-star restaurant that was hosting the event you were graciously greeted by the maître d'. He took your coat and provided you with a name tag, handwritten in graceful calligraphy. Next he escorted you as if you were some kind of international dignitary to a private party room. There a crowded reception was well under way. As you haltingly entered the room members of the mayor's committee who had made the award selections hurried to greet you. During the casual exchanges between yourself and the other guests waiters circulated with trays of hors d'oeuvres and drinks, always paying special attention to you and the other honorees. The room was beautifully decorated. Colorful flower bouquets on pedestals adorned the four corners of the reception hall. Chairs were strategically scattered around for small group conversations among the guests. A string quartet was playing Bach suites softly in the background. Tables were arranged with trays of sumptuous treats and drinks, and the well-dressed guests gave the impression of a colorful parade of pageantry and fashion.

During the actual awards ceremony the mayor publicly rehearsed your contribution and that of the other five honorees. Each of you was presented with an engraved plaque along with an unexpected monetary gift. As the mayor showcased your work in the community to those in attendance, the audience complemented his remarks with appreciative and prolonged applause. You had never been quite the center of attention like this before. Reporters circulated about the room snapping photos and conducting brief interviews. It was a gala affair.

As the evening drew to a close you gathered up the cards, gifts, plaque, and flowers you had received along with your coat. You headed to the parking lot, your arms loaded down with ceremonial loot. As you approached your car someone behind you offered, "Can I get the door for you?" As you turned around you recognized the woman making the offer. She was one of the restaurant's employees who had been serving that evening. As she opened the car door for you she congratulated you again on your work. In your effort to thank her you struck up a conversation and asked her about herself. It turned out you and she were the same age. She had worked for the restaurant for over three years. While it was a minimum wage job, she seemed to think it was pretty good pay for someone like herself. She hadn't completed high school and was grateful for a steady job with salary and tips. While it was barely enough to support herself and her two younger sisters, she remarked, "It was fine for now."

Yes, she too had enjoyed the evening. It was a welcome change from the fast-paced service in the main dining room where she usually worked. Since she had to come in early that afternoon to help with the setup and the food she was getting to go home a little early. However, it had been a long day and those tables and trays were heavy. She was tired. Smiling, she said that her greatest wish was a light snack and a good night's sleep.

The brief conversation ended. Addressing you by name, she recited again warm and sincere congratulations and you in turn expressed gratitude for her help. You wished each other a good evening and said goodbye. You hardly remember the drive home that evening. You couldn't stop thinking about this woman. There was something about her that was so sincere and gracious.

That evening you planned to watch the news when you arrived home. A local channel was expected to carry a short report as well as some footage of the evening's event. You had never been on television before. Though there was no guarantee what part of the ceremony would be aired, you secretly hoped to see yourself on the screen.

The short segment was already airing when you tuned in. There you were. Right before your viewing eyes was a two-minute clip from the awarding of honors to you. In addition, the segment carried a replay of your brief comments on receiving the award. Watching the report, you felt proud and embarrassed at the same time. Faces of others in attendance at the event appeared in the background. You couldn't help but notice the shadowy figure of a woman in uniform carrying a tray that momentarily came into focus at the edge of the screen. Though she was hard to make out amidst the crowd of faces and rapid movements of the camera, you recognized her.

\* \* \* \* \*

In this brief vignette we encounter two characters that in earlier designations would easily be labeled major and minor figures. All literary indications argue in favor of your position in the story as major character. The account of a reception held in your honor, your status as an award honoree, and your television debut cast the narrative's spotlight on you. We said earlier that at one time in literary theory a character was the sum of the words in the text about them and by them. Here the bulk of the narrative is about you. This is clearly your tale. The other player in this episode, an unnamed woman who helped you in the parking lot, would have been readily identified as a minor figure if she was even considered at all. How easy it would be to ignore this nameless figure and thereby miss the potential complexity and challenge that attention to her character discloses.

However, in contemporary literary studies on character this unnamed employee of the restaurant might, in the eyes of some readers, become a figure to be considered in depth. Studying what little the brief story tells about her, these readers might begin by considering contrasts between yourself and this figure. They might note that while you were both at the same event your experiences were quite different. You were being served while she was serving. You were in the television spotlight while she was part of the background. While everyone knew your name, no one knew who she was, not even you.

Readers intending to study her closely might draw attention to the few brief words she did say. Her passing comment that the job, with its salary and tips, "was fine *for now*" could turn out to be revelatory. Her few words here indicate that she has no intention of doing this job for life. The "for nowness" of the restaurant work suggests resignation and an acceptance of her current job status. In addition, her subsequent comment supplies the missing explanation. She is supporting her two younger sisters.

Though her remarks about herself are brief, they raise questions. Why was she, rather than her parents, supporting her siblings? Were her parents sick or deceased? Had they abandoned their children? Whatever the explanation, she had assumed responsibility for raising two younger sisters at a time when she herself was hardly an adult. That she hadn't finished high school suddenly makes new sense. Gradually any notion that would stereotype her as a high school dropout waiting on tables in a restaurant begins to fade. In its place an inkling of the woman's potential status as selfless and even heroic starts to dawn. Based upon the scant information provided by the tale, the reader begins to fill in the character of the woman. She may have been someone who had put aside herself and her plans to complete high school in order to attend to the needs of her younger sisters. Her gesture of generosity toward you in the parking lot that night coincides with this impression.

Now her character becomes immensely engaging. The example demonstrates what would be lost if the reader focused solely on the character they know most about or with whom they would most readily like to identify. Moreover, her character forms a sharp contrast to your own role as center of attention in the narrative. The dissonance here is striking. The one who privately gave up school for a minimum wage job to assume the responsibility of full-time care for two younger siblings contrasts with your prominence as a major character who was publicly honored and received a monetary gift for intermittent volunteer service. Though she is only a nameless figure with very little role to play in the narrative, her character yields immense insights and lessons from this brief scrutiny. As readers participate in building her character it poses numerous challenges for us. It raises questions especially for those of us who might more readily identify with the major character in the story. It makes us examine who the real heroes of our society are. It urges us to ponder whether we are the recipients of their generosity. It encourages inquiry within ourselves as to whether we are blind to their self-sacrifice. And it asks by what means we honor such heroes. Hence, as we confront these challenges and questions, the investigation of this woman in the narrative not only engages us in building her character. This activity and its inherent challenge to us occasion prospects for building character in us.

Similar to this woman restaurant worker, a cadre of characters who speak little, and about whom little is spoken, populate the Bible's story world. Often overshadowed by a character who is front and center in the tale, their presence in the story seems primarily functional. They constitute the background or serve as narrative aid in illuminating another character. At best their status appears adjunct in relation to the story line. As the narrator gives them little notice, we as readers tend not to notice them. Consequently they are easy to read past or ignore altogether.

For example, chapters 13 to 16 in the book of Judges are probably best known for the figure of Samson. The narrator traces an elaborate story line with Samson in the forefront. We hear accounts of his birth, his marriage, his military escapades, his romance with Delilah, and his death. Yet the words and deeds of many other characters are recorded in the course of this tale. Samson's mother and father (Judg 13:2-24), the unnamed woman from Timnah who eventually becomes his wife (14:1-20), the young men at Timnah (14:1-20), a prostitute at Gaza (16:1), the Philistines (15:6-15), and Delilah (16:4-20) all number among those who bear the weight of a story that is not theirs. These are the characters who shoulder the burden of Samson's escapades and incur the tragic consequences of his misdeeds but whom we hardly notice in the text. Because they are not accorded much attention or significance by the narrator we are less apt to identify with them. But as we will see in the following study, if we ignore such characters we do so at our own peril.

As we build characters they also build us. Our sense of ourselves and who we can become does not occur in a vacuum. It is mediated by others, and those "others" are made up not only of persons in life and characters in stories that we are quick to identify with or who seem most like us. Some of the most compelling insights about ourselves and what is possible for our lives will be prompted by those least like ourselves and by those individuals we might be trained or encouraged to ignore. Whether in life or in literature, identification with only the important figures, those with power or those crafted as the tragic or comic protagonists, breeds a fallacious understanding of ourselves. Self-understanding demands an enormous range of characters to learn from and identify with. Only then can we begin to achieve an honest assessment of our strengths and vulnerabilities, our virtues and vices, our talents and shortcomings, and our potentials and limitations. At the same time grappling with the broadest range of characters grants us urgently needed insights into the many and different "others" who make up our world and whose importance we might otherwise ignore. At this juncture in the life of our world's ever-shrinking global village the value of such knowledge and understanding needs little explanation.

## Conclusion

In this study we will explore two women and their story. According to conventional categories they are readily identified as "other," "minor," or "flat." They are nameless. That they are nameless further disqualifies their importance to the larger story in which they reside. Indeed, their own brief tale is secondary to 2 Kings 6:24-33, the larger story that dwarfs their account. Nested in the larger structure of the books of Kings, the tale these women tell is difficult. At first glance it courts revulsion.

Amidst a military siege of the city, circumstances of starvation have forced an agreement between the women to boil and eat their children. A controversy erupts between the mothers when one of them fails to make good on her word. Though it is not clear what they expect from the monarch, they set their crisis before an Israelite king. But, despite the urgent nature of their crisis, their tale is overshadowed by the apparently more dominant story, the controversy between this king and the prophet Elisha. So secondary is the mothers' tale to this larger conflict that we never even learn its ending. With the narrator's focus riveted upon the king and the prophet, the mothers' crisis goes unresolved. At best it appears as a literary prop explaining and bolstering the drama between these political and religious officials. As a result the women and their story can be readily ignored in the shadow of this seemingly more "important" set of events and characters. That they eat their children in response to this food stress further sidelines and disqualifies them as even deserving any attention.

Still, we have learned that minor characters who make us uncomfortable, who are different, or who seem less like ourselves are just as valuable for study, and sometimes more valuable than the major characters with which we more readily identify. In this study we will focus our attention on these mothers and their plight. We will refer to them as the "cannibal mothers." However, at the outset we understand that our identification of them as cannibal mothers is a characterization and not a judgment.

Like the woman in the restaurant these mothers appear at first only as fixtures, or as "the givens" in a story that is not theirs. Over and against the king and the prophet featured by the narrator these women are "the other" characters. It is only when we resist the narrator and take the time to study them up close that their real *persona* emerges.

Since the story gives them attention only in passing, we have to excavate the story line a bit more closely for hints about who they are. We can use the lens of traditional character study. How they are described, whether there is any evidence of their inner life, what they say if they speak at all, and what they do can initiate our inquiry. But we can do more. We can look for other hints in the story that can clarify their plight. We can study the king and the prophet as the contrasting characters to these women. The context of the story will also provide clues to who they are in that ancient society. Moreover, stories of other pairs of women in crisis might also be brought to bear in drafting their character and enhancing our understanding. However, as noted earlier, character studies are also cooperative ventures between readers and text. While such efforts can be casual and even unconscious, they can also be quite deliberate and calculated. Hence at times we will draw on parallels from our own experience, from the stories of women in crisis, from the plight of those persons in our world who struggle with decisions of sustenance and survival, those who confront life and death choices each day. Such an array of strategies and questions will train our attention on some textual features rather than others. We will have to concentrate our investigation on a more limited spectrum of questions having to do with these women and make inquiry upon inquiry within this narrowed field. These efforts have the advantage of a more focused and prolonged mutuality of text and reader in the process of interpretation. As a result we will be pushed deeper and deeper into the text and deeper and deeper into an understanding of these characters.

In the chapters that follow we will embark on an extended study of these cannibal mothers. Because their story unfolds in the Bible, one of the great works of literature, we will conduct our investigation under the rubric "literary criticism." Literary criticism accommodates a vast array of inquiries and practices that can be employed to study characters and their stories. From an investigation of the compositional history of a text to the analysis of the poetic artistry of a story to the discovery of the cracks, gaps, and seams in a narrative to an assessment of parallels with other tales—the scope of literary criticism as it has been played out in biblical studies is far-reaching. In Chapter Two we will set the stage for our investigation by establishing the literary terrain in which our story resides. In Chapter Three our attention will turn to three types of literary investigation. We will call these conventional literary criticism, new literary criticism, and postmodern literary criticism. We will consider how the first two of these assessments inform our reading of the cannibal mothers' story and the surrounding tale. In Chapters Four and Five we will conduct the third kind of investigation—a postmodern reading of their story and their character. In the course of these investigations we will not only learn more about these nameless women; we may also gain valuable insights and lessons for ourselves. Finally, Chapter Six will offer a conclusion, one that proposes a counter story to our cannibal mothers' tale and one that might even animate the building of character in us.

# CHAPTER TWO

## *A Story Within Stories*

In *Postscript to the Name of the Rose* Umberto Eco has written: "I've discovered what writers have always known (and have thereby told us again and again), books always speak of other books, and every story tells a story that has already been told."[1] Our story of the two cannibal mothers before a king in 2 Kings 6:24-33, the focus of this study, is no exception.

> [24]Some time later King Benhadad of Aram mustered his entire army; he marched against Samaria and laid siege to it. [25]As the siege continued, famine in Samaria became so great that a donkey's head was sold for eighty shekels of silver, and one fourth of a kab of dove's dung for five shekels of silver. [26]Now as the king of Israel was walking on the city wall, a woman cried out to him, "Help, my lord king!" [27]He said, "No! Let the LORD help you. How can I help you? From the threshing floor or from the wine press?" [28]But then the king asked her, "What is your complaint?" She answered, "This woman said to me, 'Give up your son; we will eat him today, and we will eat my son tomorrow.' [29]So we cooked my son and ate him. The next day I said to her, 'Give up your son and we will eat him.' But she has hidden her son." [30]When the king heard the words of the woman he tore his clothes—now since he was walking on the city wall, the people could see that he had sackcloth on his body underneath—[31]and he said, "So may God do to me, and more, if the head of Elisha son of Shaphat stays on his shoulders today." [32]So he dispatched a man from his presence.

---

[1] Umberto Eco, *Postscript to the Name of the Rose*, translated by William Waver (San Diego: Harcourt Brace Jovanovich, 1983–84) 20.

Now Elisha was sitting in his house, and the elders were sitting with him. Before the messenger arrived, Elisha said to the elder, "Are you aware that this murderer has sent someone to take off my head? When the messenger comes, see that you shut the door and hold it closed against him. Is not the sound of his master's feet behind him?" [33]While he was still speaking with them, the king came down to him and said, "This trouble is from the LORD! Why should I hope in the LORD any longer?"

Like a pebble dropped in a pond the little story of the cannibal mothers in 2 Kings 6:23-33 is surrounded by an ever widening circle of related stories, whole books, and eventually the entire biblical canon. However, because the Bible's story is a people's story this movement outward does not end at the confines of the biblical canon. Once set off, the ripples emanating from any biblical story move out and make contact with numerous other texts and life stories down through the ages. In subsequent chapters of this book, under the aegis of literary studies, we will follow the two mothers' story beyond its immediate literary surroundings in the second book of Kings. We will discover its echo in other stories in other biblical books. We will even read it in concert with a few stories beyond the canon until it makes its way into our own stories and lives. In the process we will make discoveries about these cannibal mothers and their tale as well as some other biblical stories, but we may even uncover more. In this trail of stories upon stories we may even arrive at new insights about ourselves.

Like any biblical account, this little tale in 2 Kings interacts not only with a variety of other texts but also with individual readers, together with what they bring to their reading. Every reader, every community, and every people coming to a text brings with them their stories, their experiences, and their past. Some of these encounters set off contrasts. At other times the life stories of readers claim kinship with a text. With each new encounter the story changes. And with each new contact the characterization of our cannibal mothers expands, enlarges, and gains new momentum, thus prompting further insights. As these stories continue to travel they eventually arrive at our doorstep and join company with our stories today.

This brief little tale takes up residence with other stories in a larger literary unit of tradition known as the Elisha cycle, which is named for the prophet Elisha. This prophetic tradition, in turn, is one of several blocks of material that together comprise the books of Kings. The books of 1 and 2 Kings, along with the books of 1 and 2 Samuel, Judges, and Joshua comprise what is commonly referred to as the Deuteronomistic History, so called because it is fashioned and imbued with the spirit of the book of

Deuteronomy. Finally, Deuteronomy, along with the other books of the Pentateuch, serves as backdrop and theological touchstone for the prophetic writings.

As we take up the story of the two cannibal mothers we begin by familiarizing ourselves with its literary surroundings. In this chapter we will consider some of those canonical environs that immediately encircle and enshrine our text. Moving from the wider context inward, we'll look briefly at the Deuteronomistic History, the books of Kings, the Elisha cycle of stories, and the immediate surrounding narrative context in 2 Kings 6:8-22 and 7:1-20 along with the story itself.

## The Deuteronomistic History

The Deuteronomistic History traces Israel's story from the conquest of Canaan to the final days of destruction and exile.[2] It begins with the book of Joshua, narrating the beginnings of Israel's comprehensive attack on the land of Canaan and the division of the land's territories among the tribes of Israel. Next the book of Judges relates Israel's configuration as a tribal society under the leaders who were called judges and the struggles of the individual tribes to maintain their land holdings. Finally, the books of Samuel and Kings map the rise of Israel to statehood. Israel thrives as a monarchy for a short period under David and Solomon. The nation's subsequent division into the northern kingdom of Israel and the southern kingdom of Judah heralds the beginning of the end. The Deuteronomistic History concludes with both nations defunct and the people stranded in exile.

Actually, the notion of a "Deuteronomistic History" is a fairly recent theory in biblical studies. For a long time the books of Joshua, Judges, 1 and 2 Samuel, and 1 and 2 Kings were viewed as independent units composed by different writers. However, in 1943 Martin Noth proposed that, taken together, these different books comprise a unified account of salvation history.[3] Considering the uniformity of the books' language and ideology, Noth argued that a single editor compiled this account. He called this writer the Deuteronomist. Working sometime during the mid-sixth century (562 B.C.E.), the Deuteronomist wove together stories, traditions, and records from the past. With theological thread he fashioned the stories according to his chosen theme of God's call for obedience and promise of judgment.

[2] For a more extended discussion of the Deuteronomistic History with commentaries to specific texts see Terence Fretheim, *Deuteronomic History*. Interpreting the Biblical Texts Series (Nashville: Abingdon, 1983).

[3] Martin Noth, *Überlieferungsgeschichtliche Studien* (Tübingen: Niemeyer, 1943).

While some scholars found Noth's proposal very appealing for a time, it did not sufficiently address some of the dissonances across these texts, particularly in regard to kingship. For example, in 1 Sam 8:10-18 the prophet Samuel warns the people that a king will impoverish them, enslave their children, and turn them away from God, yet in 10:1-2 we meet Samuel pouring a vial of oil on Saul's head, placing a kiss upon him, and proclaiming: "Has not YHWH anointed you prince over his people Israel? . . . YHWH has appointed you prince of his heritage."

A more common view, later promoted by Frank Cross and Norman Gottwald, argued for two major editions of the Deuteronomistic History. One edition originated in the time of the Judahite king, Josiah, during his acclaimed period of religious reform. The traditions assigned to this edition tended to glorify kingship and monarchy. The second edition stemmed from the exilic period after the destruction of the nation. Manifesting the wisdom of hindsight, this composition told a story of the waywardness of the kings and royalty on the road to the destruction.

Introducing this Deuteronomistic History, the preceding book of Deuteronomy establishes the theological basis for the salvation history that unfolds across these books. Cast as a series of speeches by Moses, its style is exhortation. It is hortatory in character, with a tone of urgency punctuating the rhetoric. As prelude to the Deuteronomistic work it supplies the common theological themes, ideology, literary style, and traditions that weave into a unified whole this collection of writings. The theological perspective of Deuteronomy, with its formulaic pronouncements about God's saving grace and God's judgment, permeates each of the writings. In clear, unequivocating language the Deuteronomist sets forth the choices of fidelity versus infidelity and their contrasting consequences.

> "If you will only obey the LORD your God, by diligently observing all his commandments that I am commanding you today, the LORD your God will set you high above all the nations of the earth; all these blessings shall come upon you and overtake you, if you obey the LORD your God." (28:1-2)

> "But if you will not obey the LORD your God by diligently observing all his commandments and decrees, which I am commanding you today, then all these curses shall come upon you and overtake you." (28:15)

Here and elsewhere across Deuteronomy lists of rewards in the form of blessings and litanies of punishments in the form of curses elaborate this fundamental conceptualization of Israel's relationship with God. Fidelity to God merited rewards in the form of prosperity and longevity. By contrast, infidelity, especially apostasy, guarantees judgment and punishment. Military losses, sickness, and death are some of the expressions of divine disfavor. This Deuteronomic perspective is evident throughout the entire Deuteronomistic corpus. A speech toward the conclusion of the book rehearses one last time in the gravest of terms the formulation upon which the whole Deuteronomistic History is founded.

> "See, I have set before you today life and prosperity, death and adversity. If you obey the commandments of the LORD your God that I am commanding you today, by loving the LORD your God, walking in his ways, and observing his commandments, decrees, and ordinances, then you shall live and become numerous, and the LORD your God will bless you in the land that you are entering to possess. But if your heart turns away and you do not hear, but are led astray to bow down to other gods and serve them, I declare to you today that you shall perish; you shall not live long in the land that you are crossing the Jordan to enter and possess. I call heaven and earth to witness against you today that I have set before you life and death, blessings and curses. Choose life so that you and your descendants may live . . . ." (30:15-30)

God's promise, particularly in the form of the unconditional promise of covenant to David (2 Samuel 7), is reiterated again and again across these texts. We hear echoes of the promise in the opening of the book of Judges at Joshua's death (Judg 2:1). The angel of the LORD that had gone up from Gilgal reminded the people of God's fidelity, saying, "I will never break my covenant with you." Elsewhere, when Samuel surrenders his leadership role to Saul he reminds the people of God's absolute fidelity to this promise (1 Sam 12:22). Though it is articulated somewhat differently in later traditions, David's closing words on his deathbed to his son Solomon (1 Kings 2:1-4) whisper the promise again. "If your heirs take heed to their way, to walk before me in faithfulness with all their heart and with all their soul, there shall not fail you a successor on the throne of Israel." Even years later, in the narrative record of Israel's victory over the Arameans (2 Kings 13:23), this same divine commitment still reverberates.

This frequent rehearsal of God's promise is counterbalanced by an accompanying recitation of divine judgment. The book of Judges is itself a spiraling recitation of a cycling movement—sin, judgment, punishment, and saving grace—featuring both God's judgment and God's saving grace. For example, we hear that Israel does what is displeasing before YHWH and as a consequence is enslaved by Eglon, the king of Moab. When they cry out to YHWH and repent, Ehud is raised up and delivers them from the hand of this enemy (Judg 3:12-30). Immediately following, we hear again that Israel did what was displeasing in the sight of Y H W H. As a result they are handed over to Jabin, Canaanite king at Hazor, who oppresses them. Again they cry out to Y H W H and another liberator is appointed. This time Deborah, a judge and prophet in Israel, frees them from their bondage (Judg 4:1-24).

God's abiding promise, accompanied by the guarantee of judgment for infidelity, remains constant throughout the Deuteronomistic History. No one is exempt. Even the life of the greatest king of Israel is ruled by this dynamism. Not only is David the heir to the covenantal promise: God's promise is furthered and elaborated to him and his family's line (2 Sam 7:4-16). He is promised that his descendants will never end and that his house and people will be secure forever. However, David is also subject to divine judgment. As we have already heard on one occasion, David wrongfully impregnates Bathsheba and tries to cover his tracks by having her husband, Uriah, placed in the front lines of battle. David's effort to preserve his reputation costs Uriah his life. However, David's prophet Nathan makes the king face his iniquity and recognize God's sentence. This time divine judgment visits David in the tragic death of the child of this pregnancy (2 Sam 11:1–12:23).

However, God's judgments are not ends in themselves. The Deuteronomist portrays them, instead, as a refining fire. Here one's heart is chastened, one's strength is revitalized, one's distracted mind is brought back on course, and one's soul is readied for God. God's judgment returns people to Deuteronomy's invitation to "love God with all your heart, all your soul and all your strength" so that they can be recipients of the promise—for in the end it is God's promise rather than divine judgment that shapes Israelite history and our own.

## The Books of Kings

The notion of "kings" summons images we associate with the dark ages. Crowns and scepters, castles and palaces, royal protocol and monarchs are the stuff of make-believe, children's books, movies, or even art. While most of us would reject any strong interest or desire for affiliation with royalty in our own era, there have been enough events in our own time to kindle our latent fascination with the trappings of palace life. Given the overly zealous media coverage, many of us might even admit to a mild interest in (if not rapt attention to) the celebrations, marriages, family crises, and tragedies of the British royal family.

Still, in most circles monarchs are the stuff of the past. More often than not they conjure up images of villainous or self-indulgent personalities in royal robes wielding unbridled power in word and deed. In history books they are the cause of oppression and colonization. All too often these royal figures have cost people their well-being or even their lives. In fact, the rejection of monarchic rule was the very basis upon which many of our world's democracies were founded. At best studying or even reading a book called "Kings" might be chalked up to historical interest or mere casual curiosity. The consequence of such distancing is to define these stories of power and its abuse as having little to do with us in our lives. Any expectation that there might be a message for our world today seems idle or naïve. Moreover, the line of rulers in 1 and 2 Kings is a monotonous litany that hardly qualifies as a page turner. Perhaps it requires something as jarring and unprecedented as two cannibal mothers before a king to make us take note. And when we do, we discover a challenge resident here in a most surprising way.

The books of Kings trace the line of rulers from the reign of Solomon, David's offspring, through a parade of Israelite and Judahite monarchs after the kingdom divides.[4] Though providing a framework for understanding the story of kings and the nation, the narrative across the books of Kings cannot claim to be either historically accurate or carefully arranged. The period covered (960–586 B.C.E.) extends over four hundred years, but most of the narrative report across this vast chronological span is uneven. Attention to the kings of Israel in the north far outweighs the amount of narrative describing the rulers of Judah in the south. The way in which kings came to the throne in the north versus how they ascended in the south may suggest an explanation. In Judah kings succeeded according to the Davidic line. The capital city established under David remained in Jerusalem. Hence the ascent to the throne was, for the most part, orderly and without contest. With the throne's geographical stabilization in Jerusalem there is little story left to tell.

By contrast, in the north it is unclear how kings came to reign. Initially there was no established capital. Aspiring rulers in Israel had to envision politics within the confines of the northern territories where no centralization of power or militia had been established. Many brief accounts across Kings suggest that local elites vied with other politically ambitious competitors for supremacy and public recognition. How a man gained power for himself and his clan may have had to do with the cadre of associates such a man could muster. One theory suggests that aspiring

---

[4] For a more extended study of the books of Kings see Iain Provan, *1 and 2 Kings.* New International Biblical Commentary (Peabody, Mass.: Hendrickson, 1995); Richard Nelson, *First and Second Kings.* Interpretation (Louisville: John Knox, 1987); Walter Brueggemann, *1 & 2 Kings.* Smyth and Helwys Bible Commentary (Macon, Ga.: Smyth and Helwys, 2000).

kings came into power when they were linked to powerful Yahwistic proph-ets.[5] The prophet's performance of miracles would serve as public evi-dence of YHWH's favor to that prophet and thus to the royal candidate from that clan. When a clan's bid for the throne was successful the prophets of opposing clans might perform miraculous actions that would undermine or challenge the legitimacy of their opponent who had become king.

These were not disputes politely contested. The biblical narrative teems with stories of murderous plots by power-hungry clans determined to overthrow the reigning household. Several biblical stories about prophets seem to show prophets playing a role in such situations. For example, Elisha plays an integral part in the establishment of Jehu on the throne. He appoints one from his brotherhood of prophets to go and anoint Jehu, thereby establishing him as God's choice. But in conjunction with this des-ignation of the new king the prophet also orders that the whole house of Ahab be slain. In another instance Elijah wages a contest to overpower Ahab's prophets. In the end not only is he victorious over these royal offi-cials in religious matters; Elijah also displays his military prowess when he herds the four hundred and fifty prophets down to the Wadi Kishon and slaughters them there. Across these stories prophets appear to have a very complex and significant relationship to kings in the north.

The story of kingship in Israel witnesses the coming and going of many rulers. A brief overview of the organization of these stories can lend some order to these accounts of chaos.

Three major segments of traditions craft the complex story of kingship:

> 1 Kings 1–11
> 1 Kings 12–22 and 2 Kings 1–17
> 2 Kings 18–25

1 Kings 1–11 narrates the rise and reign of Solomon. Last in the short line of three kings ruling the united monarchy (Saul, David, Solomon), Solomon's era is punctuated by massive building projects. Conscripted labor bordering on slave labor does accomplish these ambitious architec-tural feats, but it is also responsible for social unrest that eventually brings about the demise of the united nation-state. After Solomon's death the northern tribal territories secede and the nation divides into two entities—Israel in the north and Judah in the south.

---

[5] Tamara Hoover Renteria, "The Elijah/Elisha Stories: A Socio-cultural Analysis of Prophets and People in Ninth-Century B.C.E. Israel," in Robert Coote, ed., *Elijah and Elisha in Socioliterary Perspective* (Atlanta: Scholars, 1992) 76–77.

Next, 1 Kings 12–22 and 2 Kings 1–17 disclose a tumultuous period of civil strife and struggle for the survival of the now-divided nation. Ten tribes comprise Israel, the kingdom in the north. The accounts of nineteen kings within nine dynasties constantly jockeying for power occupy about eighty percent of the narrative space here. These internal contests eventually contribute to Israel's demise. The closing years record an incomparable period of murder and intrigue among want-to-be kings. During the finale, six successive rulers struggle to ascend the throne before the nation is finally destroyed by Assyria in 722 B.C.E.

The attention given to the southern kingdom of Judah and its kings is far more abbreviated. Joash's reign (837–800 B.C.E.) receives the greatest notoriety in narrative. This is both ironic and understandable since he did most to endanger the line of Davidic kings and their otherwise easy transition and ascension to the throne.

With the kingdom of Israel out of the picture 2 Kings 18–25, the third and final segment of the books, catalogues the last years of the southern kingdom. Here the narrative account slows down to spotlight the reigns of two notable rulers and their contributions, namely Josiah and Hezekiah. However, these narrative pauses are more than an interesting account of two laudable kings in Judah's history. They also set up the story of the demise of the monarchy in parallel with the story of Israel's beginnings. Israel's election as a holy people began with two decisive events: first, the call of Abraham and Sarah from their homeland in the region of Babylon to become the inheritors of a promised land; second, the liberation of Israel from their enslavement in Egypt to become the inhabitants of that promised land. Josiah instituted a comprehensive religious reform and Hezekiah rekindled relations with Babylon and Egypt. Both reigns had a defining impact on the destiny of the people. When the history of the monarchy concludes in 2 Kings 25 the nation is destroyed by Babylon and those not exiled in that foreign land seek refuge in Egypt. Sadly, though called out of Babylon and liberated from Egypt to become the chosen people, Israel now finds itself back where it started. Monarchy in Israel has yielded more than the destruction of Israel as a nation. The reign of kings has overturned and reversed the founding events of salvation history itself.

Like other biblical books, 1 and 2 Kings do not tell a separate or isolated story. They recount stories that have historical, literary, and theological connections across the larger collection of canonical works. Parallels in storytelling and other connecting devices work to tie these tales to the larger body of sacral tradition. Elijah being fed bread in the wilderness while wandering for forty days en route to Horeb (1 Kings 19), also known as Sinai, echoes the account of Moses' wilderness wanderings. David's deathbed instruction to his son Solomon hearkens back to God's covenant made with Israel's greatest king through the prophet Nathan (2 Sam 7:4-17). It reverberates back even farther to the promises made at Sinai (Exodus 19) on the heels of the Exodus event. In 1 Kings 12:28-29 Jeroboam makes two golden calves and sets them up in Bethel and Dan so the people of the new kingdom of Israel do not have to travel to Jerusalem for worship. Such events readily recall the parallel story in Exod 32:4 when Aaron fashioned a golden calf for an impatient people's homage. In such manner readers across the books of Kings are constantly reminded of these stories' connection with and participation in a larger sacred story.

Although focused almost exclusively on the royal rulers of Israel and Judah, these two books of Kings do far more than catalogue their reigns. The books raise questions, fuel suspicions, and foster skepticism about the very office of king. The overarching impression across this panorama of royal rule is that of a story gone awry. In keeping with this pervasive image of doom and gloom, the opening of 1 Kings and conclusion of 2 Kings serve as appropriate bookends defining this difficult and pessimistic account.

In 1 Kings 1–2 this parade of monarchs opens with the death of a king. David, the united kingdom's greatest monarch, is on his deathbed, hardly aware of his surroundings. Though he is succeeded by his son Solomon, David's legacy is immediately marked by the bloodstained trail in the course of Solomon's ascension to power. The chapters that follow across these two books are marked by similar recurrent scrimmages for domestic dominion along with contests for international power. When the story closes, kings and their kingdoms have been destroyed. The united kingdom and the divided kingdoms no longer stand. The people have been dispersed or are in exile. The sole survivor of the Davidic line is in Babylonian captivity and only recently released from the humiliation of imprisonment.

Scattered across this panorama of political combat and collapse are fleeting references to the lives and destinies of individual citizens, lives obscured and aborted in the wake of the disastrous melee. Our tale of the two cannibal mothers before a king is but one example. It illustrates the plight of persons rendered insignificant in the wake of kings and their schemes. It marks members of a society whose futures could be sacrificed. Moreover, as our study of these cannibal mothers will show, it suggests how life itself becomes a negotiated commodity when power is at stake.

## Prophets and Kings

The course and outcome of these stories about monarchy may make one wonder why books such as Kings are counted among the works of the canon of Sacred Scripture. On what grounds do these writings claim to re-count salvation history? Interestingly, while the Christian canon designates these writings as part of the historical books, the *Tanakh* or Hebrew Bible lists 1 and 2 Kings among the writings it earmarks as "Former Prophets." The fact that prophets are crucial to kings throughout these narratives ex-plains this categorization within the Jewish Scriptures. Prophets both sup-port kings and are critical of kings. They are consulted by kings and viewed as threats by kings. More often than not the words the prophets speak and their interpretation of events from God's viewpoint form a sharp contrast and alternative to what kings say and what they do. With the prophets bringing God's word to bear on every crisis throughout the monar-chic history it is easy to see why these books might just as reasonably be designated prophets' stories as historical writings.

Across these two books of Kings prophets emerge as the contrasting counterpart to kings. At the beginning of these tales David's prophet, Nathan, figures prominently in the close of David's reign and the rise of Solomon to power. Unable to make a decision about a successor, David must be coerced by Nathan in order for Solomon to ascend the throne (1 Kings 1:11-35). When the united kingdom ends after the reign of Solomon the prophet Ahijah is instrumental in bringing this first era to a close (1 Kings 11:29-43). Toward the conclusion of these books Micaiah and some other prophets have a role to play. Micaiah, son of Imlah and prophet of the northern kingdom, foresees the defeat and death of Ahab in the battle with the Arameans at Ramoth-gilead (1 Kings 22:8-28). Huldah, a woman prophet in the south, is consulted by King Josiah as to the con-tents of a law book found during the Temple's renovation. Upon her inter-pretation of this text the king institutes a comprehensive religious reform (1 Kings 23). We also hear from Isaiah of Jerusalem (2 Kings 19–20), who is a major consultant as well as healer to King Hezekiah. Later in the canon we encounter a whole book assigned to the prophet Isaiah, where his words and works are more extensively catalogued.

Hence what appears to be the tale of kings is also, at the same time, the story of prophets. As counselors of kings, prophets inform Israel's rulers of God's will and ways. As opponents of these royal sovereigns, prophets chastise and admonish kings for their waywardness and infidelity. Unfortunately, the clashes outnumber the collaborations between these po-litical and religious officials. Hence the books of Kings are not only about kings jockeying for power and control with other candidates for the throne at home, nor are they dominated solely by Israel's kings in strife with inter-national adversaries who threaten domestic well-being. The books of Kings must also be described as stories of clashes and conflicts between kings and prophets. Prophets as heralds of God's word emerge as the contrasting prototype to kings in all their waywardness.

## The Elisha Tradition

Nested within the very center of these books of Kings are the accounts of the activities of two related prophets, Elijah and Elisha. The tales of these two men of God living and working in the northern kingdom dominate the second portion of the narrative (1 Kings 12–22; 2 Kings 1–17). While the books of Kings give special attention to this period, much of this attention is focused on stories about these two prophets. Elijah's stories are interwoven across 1 Kings 17–2 Kings 2. The stories of Elisha, his successor, begin where Elijah's narrative ends. Beginning in 2 Kings 2 and extending through chapter 13, Elisha's stories conclude with an account of his death (13:14-21). It is within this cycle of Elisha stories that our tale of the two cannibal mothers unfolds. And it is within the context of a contest between a king and a prophet that the conflict between these two mothers develops.

Elisha's work as a prophet, which straddles the ninth to eighth centuries, spans a period of some seventy years encompassing the reigns of the northern kings Ahaziah, Joram, Jehu, Joahaz, and Joash (850–780 B.C.E.). We first hear of Elisha in 1 Kings 19:16 when Elijah, who has sought to preserve his life in the wilderness, is instructed to go back and anoint Elisha as his successor. When Elijah goes to call on him Elisha is plowing behind twelve yoke of oxen. Elijah casts his cloak over the man, and Elisha responds by following the prophet and becoming his servant (1 Kings 19:19-21).

The story of Elisha, who is introduced as the son of Shaphat of Abel-Meholah, unfolds across 2 Kings 2–13. While most of his stories are confined to 2 Kings 2–8, the prophet also appears briefly in the revolt of Jehu (2 Kings 9:1-3) and in the brief account of Elisha's own last days and death (2 Kings 13:14-21). His story opens with Elisha witnessing his predecessor Elijah's ascent to heaven in a whirlwind (2 Kings 2:11). Understanding himself as successor, Elisha requests and receives double the portion of Elijah's spirit for the tasks ahead. Such a request and its meaning have always been a curiosity for interpreters. Often it is understood as a humble gesture on the part of Elisha reflecting awareness of the greatness of his predecessor Elijah. However, in light of study of the cannibal mothers we might consider Elisha's request as indication of his own perception of inadequacy for the job ahead.

The Elisha tradition is as vast as the varied stories crafting it. The following list catalogues the individual tales in 2 Kings that together comprise this prophetic cycle:

2:19-22    Elisha purifies the water.
2:23-25    Elisha curses the small boys.
3:11-20    Elisha advises Jehoram, king of Israel, and Jehosaphat,
          king of Judah, in their campaign against Moab.
4:1-7      Elisha multiplies oil on behalf on a widow.
4:8-37     Elisha raises the son of a Shunammite woman.
4:38-41    Elisha purifies the poisoned soup for the brotherhood of
          prophets.
4:42-44    Elisha multiplies loaves and vegetables for the company of
          prophets.
5:1-20     Elisha cures the leprosy of Naaman.
5:21-27    Elisha punishes Gehazi, his servant, for an act of deception.
6:1-7      Elisha rescues the iron ax head from the Jordan.
6:8-23     Elisha deceives and captures a band of Arameans.
6:24-33    Elisha is in conflict with the king over the famine in besieged
          Samaria.
7:1-26     Elisha's prediction that the siege will end materializes.
8:1-6      Elisha restores all that belongs to the Shunammite woman.
8:7-15     Elisha counsels Hazael that he will become king of Aram.
9:1-10     Elisha anoints Jehu king in Israel.
13:14-17   Elisha predicts Jehoash's victory over Damascus.
13:20-21   Elisha dies and a dead man who touches the dead prophet's
          bones is resurrected.

At first glance we are struck by the rich reservoir of popular tales about practical as well as political matters. The stories of the multiplication of the widow's oil, the raising of a Shunammite woman's son, and Elisha's cure of Naaman's leprosy fashion an image of the prophet caught up in providing food, healing, and well-being to the rural populace at large. In addition, stories of his purification of poisonous soup for the prophets' meal, multiplication of loaves and vegetables for another group, and the rescue of the ax from the Jordan for his brother prophets disclose Elisha's concern for the needs and well-being of an assembly of prophets. Further, Elisha's interaction with kings and their dependence upon him indicate activities that eclipse the confines of village life or even the concerns of the brotherhood of prophets. The scope of the Elisha stories suggests the wide range of his influence.

The group of stories making up this prophetic tradition not only provides insight into the world and work of this particular prophet; it also affords a good sampling of the kinds of activities that typify the prophets. Not only were they involved with the life of the common people; often prophets were sought out by kings for counsel. They confronted rulers with their political waywardness as well as their personal misdeeds. Moreover, the prophets' involvement in these social and political situations was not confined to national problems or to their own rulers. Their pronouncements embroiled them in disputes not only at home but with foreign rulers. In addition, such exchanges were not without complications. Prophets had to constantly weigh and make choices about the common good and morally acceptable courses of action. At times they fared very well. At other times they were ostracized for their words and deeds. What is more, like all human beings they had to struggle with their own ambitions and inclinations—the kind that could render their counsel and their actions questionable or lamentable. In the best of circumstances they stood as trustworthy advocates of the word and way of the LORD. In the worst of circumstances they were capable of looking just like the political officials whose tactics they decried or even sought to counter.

Elijah, for example, is embroiled in a conflict with King Ahab for the way this king has been putting YHWH's prophets to the sword and leading the people of Israel away from their God. When the prophet confronts this king he not only condemns him for promoting the worship of the foreign god Baal but also denounces his royal policies for ordering the murderous destruction of YHWH's prophets. Nevertheless, in a victorious moment on Mt. Carmel, Elijah himself orders all the prophets of Baal to be brought down to the Wadi Kishon, where he slaughters them (1 Kings 18:40). This murderous finale causes the prophet to look a lot like the political ruler he condemns. Nathan, bent upon securing Solomon as David's heir to the throne, employs a deceitful scheme to secure the ailing king's cooperation. Though he successfully foils Adonijah's preemptive strike, Nathan stoops to deception in order to accomplish his goal. Again the prophet employs the same despicable tactics as the rulers he often condemns. On this score Elisha is no exception. Elisha's encouragement of Hazael to assassinate his lord (8:9-10) is troublesome and disturbing. Moreover, the prophet's counsel to Jehu to assassinate not only the reigning king but the king's entire family certainly gives the reader pause.

Prophets, as deliverers of the word of God, carry a lot of weight. They are very influential persons within both political and religious circles. On that score they are a lot like their royal counterparts, whose position of influence also invests them with a great deal of power. Ironically, prophets, like their contrasting royal counterparts, must constantly wrestle with and confront the dangers and pitfalls of power. Like kings, they too are capable of succumbing to these perils. Hence confrontations between kings and prophets are not just testy committee meetings about political or religious issues. In these encounters between kings and prophets, prestige and power are often at stake.

This is precisely the framework of the story world of our tale and its surrounding context. In the narrative of the two cannibal mothers before a king, the prophet and the king of Israel are embroiled in a conflict. Like bookends, the tales that immediately precede and follow the mothers' story help illuminate their opposition. However, as we will see, these stories also further complicate and extend the scope of the prophet's influence and conflict. The conflict between Israel and Syria in the story that precedes also tells us that Elisha and the forces of Syria are opponents. At the same time, Israel's king and the prophet are at odds. Hence these struggles for power and networks of influence are enmeshed and convoluted. In such circumstances political as well as religious allegiances are not easy to define. Thus, as we shall see, those entwined in these struggles are susceptible to compromise and corruption.

## Surrounding Narrative Context and the Story of the Two Cannibal Mothers

Two related stories (6:8-22 and 7:1-20) frame our tale of the two cannibal mothers before a king. In the first story Elisha dupes the Syrian army and then sets them free. In the second account Elisha's prediction that the Syrian siege will end and the famine will be over comes about. In both accounts the prophet Elisha is instrumental in causing the Syrian army to be shamed, as we will see. Immediately we are struck by the parallel governing the stories surrounding our narrative. In both of these the prophet wields power and, as a result, Israel and its king hold sway in relation to the Syrian army. However, these narrative environs contrast sharply with the story they enclose in 2 Kings 6:24-33. In our story Israel is enclosed within its walls, surrounded and beset by the Syrian forces. At the same time the prophet has enclosed himself in his house, beset by a threat to his life by Israel's king. Here Israel and its king are held captive and the prophet is dodging threats to his life. These parallels and contrasts structure the literary network within which we read our story. First we will consider the account that precedes and acts as prelude. Next we will take up our story. Finally we will attend to the account of events that acts as the closing framework.

### *1 Kings 6:8-23*

The story in 6:8-23 introduces us to the conflict between Israel and the Syrian army and forms a contrasting prelude to our tale. It sketches an account of the prophet's response to the ambitions of the Syrian king, who is bent on war with Israel. As the episode opens details are scant. No date situates these unfolding events. No reason explains why the Syrian monarch is planning this assault against Israel. No hint indicates where his armies are encamped. Moreover, the very identity of this king is glaringly absent. The silence surrounding all this seemingly pertinent information suggests that the heart of this story lies beyond these details. Instead, Elisha is apparently the intended centerpiece of this account. The prophet demonstrates he has inside knowledge of the Syrian plan and informs Israel's king of the impending attack. Hence even before the Syrian army has a chance to exercise its might it is foiled by the prophet's guile.

Outraged that his military plan has been frustrated, the Syrian king first suspects a traitor among his own men. When it becomes clear that Israel's "man of God" has uncovered his scheme Elisha replaces Israel as the Syrian's target for military capture. The Syrian army will kidnap the prophet. In this way the foreign king and his army put an end to Elisha's "military intelligence" that seems privy to even conversations in the Syrian king's bedroom. Without narrative delay the prophet and his servant are surrounded at Dothan by the Syrian army. In contrast to the cool, calm, and self-assured demeanor of Elisha, the prophet's servant panics and expresses his despair. On seeing the surrounding Syrian army ready to attack, he exclaims to Elisha, "'Alas, master! What shall we do?'" (6:15). Elisha responds by comforting the servant, affording him a glimpse of his own prophetic vision. This momentary disclosure shows that the Syrian army is in fact surrounded by Elisha's own militia, horses, and chariots of fire.

Now the story shifts from a vision to a prayer. The prophet prays that the invading enemy be struck with a kind of blindness, literally "bedazzlement." Immediately his request is granted. The Syrian soldiers' obscured vision prevents these intruders from recognizing the prophet. Moreover, it also makes them receptive to following him. Elisha now adds insult to injury and leads the Syrian army right into Samaria, where they are quickly surrounded by the Israelite forces. Elisha has completely turned the tables on the Syrian army as well as turned the story around. The Syrian ploy to kidnap the prophet at Dothan has been undercut by the prophet's ruse. The Syrian army's effort to capture Israel has resulted in Israel's seizure of the Syrian army.

In his enthusiasm for this most remarkable turn of events, Israel's king seizes this unearned opportunity for power. He immediately readies the order to have the prisoners executed. However, the prophet's incredible display of power indicates that he is in charge. Elisha counters the king's execution plan with an order that the men be fed and sent on their way. Though we might think this a gesture of compassion, more likely it serves as a stinging blow of humiliation in an ancient cultural system of honor and shame. How much more honorable is it to be killed by the enemy in battle than to be taken prisoner by them and then sent home!

That the king of Israel concurs with the prophet's plan and releases the men suggests more than agreement about military tactics. The king's compliance discloses the influence and power of the prophet in the unfolding events. However, with power and influence at stake among such public figures as kings and prophets this cooperation will not last long. In the following tale of the cannibal mothers before a king the compliance will fade. The conflict between prophet and Syrian king will be matched and compounded by a further conflict—this time between Elisha and Israel's king.

### The Story of the Two Cannibal Mothers before a King: 2 Kings 6:24-33

Our story opens with "some time later," drawing a sequential connection between what has preceded and what follows. However, in the same opening sentence we are provided information that creates a disjunction with what has gone before our account. The Syrian king and his army that Israel had besieged in the previous tale have now "marched against Samaria and laid siege to it" (6:24). Hence as the story opens we are not only aware that Israel's victory over Syria has been reversed but that the content of our story confines this episode and its characters within the walls of the city of Samaria, Israel's capital. It begins by reporting that Ben-hadad, an Aramean (Syrian) king, has surrounded Samaria and thus is holding its inhabitants captive. Though no historical context or circumstances are specified, it is easy to imagine what prompted this comprehensive display of power. Israel's capital Samaria has been attacked in response to the humiliation of the Syrian army that was captured, fed, and sent home. In a massive, uncompromising strike Ben-Hadad seizes Samaria, surrounds it, and prevents all commerce going in or out. This action inflicts great hardship on the people confined there. The consequences of the military assault are detailed in the report that follows.

The gravity of these wartime circumstances materializes most graphically in the marketplace. Famine is wreaking havoc in the city. On the economic front foods that are unsavory, if not inedible, are commanding exorbitant prices. In the best of times an ass's head would be the least desirable of meats for consumption. A poor person might gather dove's dung as a desperate way to recover precious undigested seed for cultivation of food.[6]

---

[6] Numerous proposals have been made for the translation and understanding of ass's head and dove's dung as food items. See Gwilym Jones, *1 and 2 Kings*. New Century Bible Commentary 2 (Grand Rapids: Eerdmans, 1984) 431–32 for a summary of these discussions.

That such substances are commanding ridiculous prices in the marketplace suggests the gravity of the economic crisis resulting from the siege. In turn such an assault on this city's economic well-being gives way to unthinkable desperation on the domestic front. A shift from third-person description on the part of the narrator to first-person speech on the part of characters magnifies and personalizes the gravity of the situation.

With the salutation familiar across the biblical tradition, an unidentified woman beseeches the unnamed Israelite ruler who is walking on the city's wall (6:26). Without introduction or invitation she cries, "Help, my lord king!" Most likely this is King Jehoram, ruler in Israel at this desperate time. Without any inquiry the monarch responds. He assumes that the woman seeks relief from the widespread conditions of starvation. He confesses his inability to help but absolves himself of responsibility for her suffering by defining the wine press and the threshing floor as God's domain (6:27). When finally allowed to specify her request, the woman describes a different crisis, one that stems from the conditions of starvation but far exceeds them in gravity (6:28-29). An unthinkable controversy has erupted between herself and another mother since they agreed to eat their children together, one child after the other. They have already boiled and consumed this woman's child, but now the other woman has broken the pact and hidden her offspring. What this woman is requesting of the king remains unclear. She may be asking him to require the other woman to make good on her word. She may be relating the circumstances of the quarrel between herself and the other woman as illustration of how bad things have become. Or she may be seeking a remedy for the severity of their crisis from the only one who might still have the power to save them.[7]

The king's response to the woman is twofold. He tears his robe. This public gesture of lament familiar in the ancient world reveals something more. "The people could see that he had sackcloth on his body underneath" (6:30). Second, and in the same moment, the king pronounces a vow to kill Elisha, the prophet of God, whom the king evidently holds responsible for the conditions of starvation (6:31). Immediately the focus of the tale shifts to the prophet and his dwelling.

---

[7] Some scholars argue that the woman's appeal, "Help, my lord king!" is a legal address requesting the king's judicial arbitration. See Mordecai Cogan and Hayim Tadmor, *II Kings.* AB 11 (New York: Doubleday, 1988) 79; Stuart Lasine, "Jehoram and the Cannibal Mothers (2 Kings 6.24-33): Solomon's Judgment in an Inverted World," *JSOT* 50 (1991) 48; James Montgomery, *The Books of Kings.* International Critical Commentary (New York: Scribner's, 1957) 358. However, the king's initial response in 6:27 does not indicate that he understands her salutation as a legal request. On the contrary, he confesses his lack of power and blames God.

Elisha is in his house in the company of the elders. Aware of the king's intentions and the messenger the king has sent, Elisha orders the doors of his house to be barred shut (6:32). There is some confusion over the translation in the next sentence (6:33). The conversation that ensues in 6:33–7:1 suggests that the king, rather than his messenger, journeys to the prophet's house. In Hebrew the word for "the messenger" (*hammal'ak*) that appears in the ancient Masoretic text is very similar to the word for "the king" (*hammel'ek*). The interchange that follows between king and prophet, along with the very real possibility of a scribal error, argues in favor of reading that "the king" himself has come to the prophet's door. When he arrives the king has apparently come to his senses and retreats from his threat. Without explanation we learn that the king has a change of heart. He attributes the present conditions to YHWH and confesses his despair (6:33). Hence the story ends with a resolution of the conflict between king and prophet.

## 2 Kings 7:1-20

In the story that follows our tale of the cannibal mothers the siege is resolved upon Elisha's word (7:1-20). As the story opens, the prophet declares that both meal and barley will be available the next day for a very meager price in the market. In addition Elisha promises that the king's captain will witness this shift in circumstances but not have occasion to eat from this new abundance. Next, four lepers enter the narrative. Without introduction they stand in the city's gateway contemplating their fate. They decide that deserting to the Syrian forces might be their greatest chance at life. However, when they arrive at the strongholds surrounding Samaria they find the Syrian camp deserted. The narrative offers a parenthetical explanation.

> YHWH had caused the Syrian army to hear the sound of chariots, and of horses, the sound of a great army, so that they said to one another, "The king of Israel has hired the kings of the Hittites and the kings of Egypt to fight against us." So they fled away in the twilight and abandoned their tents, their horses, and their donkeys leaving the camp just as it was, and fled for their lives. (7:6-8)

On seeing that the camp is deserted the lepers eat, drink, and then loot two tents. However, no sooner have they begun their nighttime carouse than they have some second thoughts about culpability if their nocturnal jaunt were to be discovered in the morning. Hence they decide to inform Israel's king of the Syrian retreat.

Upon hearing the news Israel's king acts like any prudent military leader. He suspects a trap on the part of the Syrian forces. In consultation with some of his advisors he decides to send horses and chariots into the camp as decoys to rule out the possibility of the Syrian army hiding in wait. When no ambush occurs, the king is convinced that indeed the Syrians have deserted in haste.

Immediately the captive people of Samaria begin pouring out of the besieged city and plundering the Syrian camp. They carry off all the remaining supplies and foodstuffs. The markets can now reopen in Samaria, supplied with abundant spoils from the enemy encampments. As the prophet foretold, now two measures of barley can be bought for a mere shekel and a measure of fine grain for about the same. Also as the prophet foretold, the king's "captain" at the gate witnesses the resolution of the famine but does not live to partake in the new abundance. As this little episode closes we hear that "the people trampled him to death in the gate" (7:20). Again the power of the prophet's word is made manifest, but at the expense of an unnamed citizen.

## Summary and Conclusion

True to the character of the Deuteronomistic History and the books of Kings, both the tale of the cannibal mothers and the surrounding stories narrate conflicts between kings and prophets. In the stories that precede and follow our tale the prophet is at odds with a foreign king and works to overturn the enemy's scheme. In the first confrontation the prophet acts to humiliate and topple the foreign ruler. In the second Elisha reveals God's word, which brings about the overturning of the Syrian assault. Juxtaposed between these stories of hostility is the tale of the two cannibal mothers before a king. Here the prophet and Israel's king are opponents.

Dwarfed in relationship to the king and prophet, confined within the walls of the city, and embedded in a story line that never gets completed, the tale of the cannibal mothers lacks luster. It dwindles in importance when compared with the military crisis the king faces, which threatens the whole city. It fades in its urgency alongside the challenge facing the prophet, that is, to foil the Syrian assault. Whether it should even be called "the tale" of the two cannibal mothers is a reasonable question. After all, their crisis is not the main crisis of the story. We have no information about who the mothers are or anything about their background. In fact, we don't even know how the mothers' crisis was resolved. At best their story seems to function as a mere literary prop. It appears to join with other stories, forming the thematic backdrop of a larger tale. This backdrop sketches the life threatening lack of food in Samaria. In the complex of the narrative that follows, the episode of the cannibal mothers can be subsumed into a category of references that portray these prevailing ecological conditions of starvation. The high prices in the marketplace, Elisha's prediction of a decrease in food prices by the morrow, the urgent hunger expressed by the lepers, and the stampede for food at the end join with the episode of the cannibal mothers to serve as background against which the main plot of the story is painted. The mothers' controversy, their starvation, their desperation, and the threat to the second child's life are never addressed, never resolved, never returned to in the grander literary scheme. Their concerns are not the concerns of the larger narrative. Without a doubt this is a story that is secondary to the larger story—the story of kings and prophets.

That these mothers qualify as "secondary" or "minor" characters according to most literary conventions is indisputable. That they are nameless makes them easy to ignore. That they would boil and eat their children makes them reprehensible and easy to blame. How we might learn anything about ourselves or our society by studying such minor characters is a real question. Can we really assert that they challenge the violent currents of our own time as well as illuminate our own self-understanding in regard to violence? That remains to be seen.

# CHAPTER THREE

## Literary Criticism and the Tale of Two Cannibal Mothers

Because the biblical writings rank among the world's greatest literary achievements it is no surprise that *literary criticism* has become common-place in the study of these texts. Discriminating appreciation of literature along with the pursuit of meaning within a literary work invites and even demands this kind of scrutiny. That the Bible's status as great literature in-vites this kind of investigation is not a recent discovery. The very estab-lishment of a biblical canon suggests that even the ancient church itself was practicing a kind of literary criticism. The process of discerning which books to include in the canon likely occasioned some consideration of the literary unity and integrity of these writings.

As early as the first century the Jewish philosopher Philo was writing about literary features such as rhythm and meter within the song of Moses (Exodus 15).[1] Among the early church fathers Jerome, in his comparison of Roman and biblical literature, was investigating matters of style, tone, and rhetoric.[2] From earliest times Jewish rabbis were immersed in discussions of poetic devices such as repetitions, gaps, and key words in their study and interpretations of the biblical writings.[3] Hence the practice of a so-called

---

[1] Philo, *De Vita Mosis*, translated by F. H. Colson. Vol. 6 *Loeb Classical Library* (Cam-bridge, Mass.: Harvard University Press, 1966) 1.23.

[2] H.F.D. Sparks, "Jerome as Biblical Scholar," in P. R. Ackroyd and C. F. Evan, eds., *Cambridge History of the Bible. Vol. 1: From the Beginnings to Jerome* (Cambridge: Cam-bridge University Press, 1970) 510–41.

[3] Shaye J. D. Cohen, *From Maccabees to Mishnah* (Philadelphia: Westminster, 1987) 200–13; Tzvee Zahavy, "Biblical Theory and Criticism: Midrash and Medieval Commentary," in Michael Groden and Martin Kreiswirth, eds., *Johns Hopkins Guide to Literary Theory and Criticism* (Baltimore: Johns Hopkins University Press, 1994) 81–84.

literary criticism, though not yet recognized as a practice with regard to the biblical texts, seems to have coincided with and been prompted by the very development of these writings themselves.

In recent years the discipline of biblical studies has formalized its literary study of these texts. Criticisms, or the various approaches to investigating the biblical writings as literature, have served to systematize these inquiries. The crisis of credibility that the Enlightenment posed to religion in general, and to such enterprises as biblical studies in particular, encouraged the formalization of these criticisms. The strictures of positivism demanded the kind of evidence and argumentation that would shape the mindset and methods of subsequent generations of biblical scholars and their work.

In this chapter we will take up the complex matter of literary criticism as it has been and continues to be conducted in biblical studies today. However, any expectations of a neat and tidy definitive step-by-step approach called "literary criticism" will be quickly frustrated. Instead we will discover that the notion of literary criticism has meant many different kinds of analyses of texts. We will organize this diversity of approaches by considering three significant turns that the tradition of interpretation has taken in the matter of literary criticism over the past two hundred years in biblical studies. We will label these developmental shifts "conventional literary criticism," "new literary criticism," and "postmodern literary criticism."

In reviewing these shifts we will rehearse the development and features of conventional literary criticism first and then that of new literary criticism. In each case a description of the objective and method of each mode of analysis will guide the discussion. An assessment of our text, the two cannibal mothers before a king (2 Kings 6:24-33), will follow each of these descriptions. In the process the contours of these first two modes of criticism will be illustrated along with how each one illuminates the interpretation of our text. An exploration of the development and objectives of postmodern literary studies will follow. This approach, with its attention to the underside of stories, its preoccupation with other voices in the text, and its fascination with the fragmentary, plural, contradictory, and heterogeneous elements of a tale will prove to be an essential lens for our character study of the two cannibal mothers in the next chapter. Hence the conclusion, with its discussion of postmodern literary criticism, will prepare us for the analysis of our story in the chapter that follows.

## Traditional Literary Criticism

During the eighteenth century the Enlightenment Period instigated a crisis of credibility that prompted the beginning of the reign of historical critical studies among biblical scholars. Determined to respond to the demands of empiricism and rationalism, German scholars in particular often argued that the investigation of the biblical text and also biblical theology itself must be grounded in the datum of history. Literary criticism, what German scholars called *Literarkritik,* featured prominently in this objective. In concert with the purpose of historical studies, literary criticism of the Bible investigated and traced the compositional history of the text. It was concerned with the sources, the changes to the materials as they were handed down from generation to generation, the editions, and the final compositional process. However, these interests were not merely excavative, nor were these pursuits considered a turning away from the characteristic concerns of literary studies.

Like the conventional practices conducted in literature departments across the academy, conventional literary criticism of the Bible during the nineteenth and early twentieth centuries also attended to poetic features of the writing. Stylistic devices, themes, key expressions, and viewpoint were some of the numerous foci of these investigations. Considerations of a passage's structure and organization or whether it manifests literary unity occupied attention. However, interest in these literary elements was not an end in itself; rather it was the means to achieving another end. The compositional history of the text defined and determined this overarching objective of biblical literary criticism. Hence literary features of the biblical writings such as point of view, stylistics, poetics, etc., became not the basis for an interpretation but the supporting evidence of the historical status of the text. The presence of different literary styles or themes or viewpoints within such books as Exodus or Numbers provided grounds for arguing the presence of two or more sources contributing to a text's composition. Difference in theological images, ideological emphasis, or changes in the names of persons and places served as evidence for the establishment of particular periods and contexts for these sources.

During the first half of the twentieth century Julius Wellhausen's monumental documentary hypothesis became the most familiar exemplar of literary criticism.[4] Wellhausen and others with him studied the language and style of texts, the formulaic language in poetry, and such aesthetic features as the presence of rhetorical questions, repetition, parallelisms, and contrasts in vocabulary. Continuities and discontinuities in the story line, shifts in theological constructions, and variances in ethical positions became

---

[4] Julius Wellhausen, *Prolegomena to the History of Ancient Israel.* With a Preface by W. Robertson Smith (Edinburgh: Adam & Charles Black, 1885; repr. New York: Meridian, 1957).

the data of his literary assessment. However, these literary scrutinies were not ultimately about the interpretation of the text. Such assessments were but a first stage in the service of a larger purpose, discovering the history of the text and its composition.

For example, an in-depth study of Genesis 1–2 offers an immense yield of literary devices and styles for assessment. At first glance two distinct literary styles, theologies, and emphases can be noted. Genesis 1:1–2:4a exhibits explicit poetic elements such as repetition, parallelism, and a highly organized format that structures the account of creation across the span of seven days. Here the only glimpse we get of God is in the form of divine *fiat:* "And God said . . . ." By contrast, in Gen 2:4b-25 narrative prose supplants the preceding poetic repetitive recitation. Here God is highly anthropomorphized, a busy potter crafting humans from the earth's clay and breathing life into that which is made. Here humans are fashioned first, in contrast to the previous story where humans are the concluding act of creation. A Hebrew word play establishes the relationship between the earth creature *(ha'adam)* and the earth *(ha'adamah)* out of which the creature is made until God breathes divine breath into this *'adam*. In contrast to the repetitive framework of the poem describing creation in 1-2:4a, this account qualifies as prose and narrates a story of creation. But for Wellhausen such literary assessments are not ends in themselves. Instead they become indicators of the compositional history of this text, arguing for at least two sources for these stories. And as the analysis continues across Genesis, Exodus, Leviticus, Numbers, and Deuteronomy the catalogue of literary observations mushrooms and in turn provides hard evidence for a source hypothesis explaining the compositional history of the five books of the Pentateuch.

Founded upon such data, the now familiar proposal by Wellhausen argues that four major sources were brought together in the composition of the Pentateuch. As each of the four sources was isolated across these five books, textual elements such as their language, theological emphasis, and geographical references became the grounds for further investigation and hypotheses regarding the context and time period for the origin of each strand.[5] Thus literary criticism was at the service of historical studies. Literary artistry became hard evidence for historical proposals and the literary text was mined for evidence of historical context.

As the biblical writings began to function as historical evidence that identified the text with a particular time period and context, they soon were

---

[5] For an introduction to Wellhausen's findings and how each source becomes distinguished by way of its literary features see Walter Brueggemann and Hans Walter Wolff, *The Vitality of the Old Testament Traditions* (Atlanta: John Knox, 1982).

put to use serving another of history's interests. With composition tied to a particular time period and context, the biblical writings became a window into that historical era. This type of criticism centered around the assessment of the truth or accuracy of the text as reflection. How the text might serve as a reflection on the context of one of its compositional phases was considered. For example, the ancestor period in Israel to which the Abraham and Sarah stories in Genesis are tied dates to approximately 2000–1800 B.C.E. However, a study of the literary features of some of the Abraham and Sarah traditions suggested that they were written and edited approximately 950 B.C.E., around the time of Solomon's reign as king in Israel. Hence these stories about the ancestors serve less as evidence of the ancestor period about which they are written. Rather, they function as a valuable reflection of some of the reigning social practices, linguistic expressions, or perhaps even notions of God of the later monarchic era of Solomon's time. Hence literary assessment of the Pentateuchal writings yielded information not only about compositional history but also about the context of that compositional setting.

Though immensely fruitful in the study of the Pentateuch, this conventional literary criticism was not confined to those books. The Deuteronomistic History, the prophetic writings, and even such Wisdom texts as Job underwent this kind of compositional scrutiny. The books of Kings, where our story of the cannibal mothers resides, have been the subject of numerous literary assessments and proposals as to their sources and compositional history.[6] This kind of excavative study was not restricted to large segments of the canon or even to whole books. Individual sagas, novellas, legends, and stories that make up these books were also targets for study then and they still are the focus of such inquiry in some circles today.

For example, the Elisha tradition, which includes our story of the cannibal mothers, has been the subject of numerous literary investigations—all

---

[6] The scope and endurance of this debate is represented in the following small sample of studies. See Immanuel Benzinger, *Jahvist und Elohist in den Königsbüchern.* BWAT n.s. 2 (Berlin, Stuttgart, and Leipzig: Kohlhammer, 1921); Frank M. Cross, "The Themes of the Books of Kings and the Structure of the Deuteronomistic History," in his *Canaanite Myth and Hebrew Epic: Essays in the History and Religion of Israel* (Cambridge, Mass.: Harvard University Press, 1973); Gustav Hölscher, "Das Buch der Könige, seine Quellen und seine Redaktion," in *Eucharisterion Hermann Gunkel zum 60. Geburtstag.* FRLANT 36 (Göttingen: Vandenhoeck & Ruprecht, 1927); Richard D. Nelson, *The Double Redaction of the Deuteronomistic History.* MSSOTS 18 (Sheffield: Sheffield University Press, 1981); Martin Noth, *Überlieferungsgeschichtliche Studien: Die sammelnden und bearbeitenden Geschichtswerke im Alten Testament* (2nd ed. Tübingen: Mohr, 1957); Julius Wellhausen, *Die Composition des Hexateuchs und der historischen Bücher des Alten Testaments* (Berlin: Georg Reimer, 1889).

in the interest of establishing sources, history of composition, and eventually context. The assessment of the literary features has been lucrative. Many studies assessing the materials spanning 2 Kings 2–9 argue for two main sources from which this cycle of stories making up this prophetic tradition is drawn.[7] A pool of stories about the prophet constituted the first proposed source. Recorded historical narrative was earmarked as the second source.

Once again, however, the assessments of contributing literary features and components were not an end in themselves. Rather, the presence of these components across the Elisha traditions served as a basis for the two source proposals. A collation of literary features in some of the Elisha stories supported the designation of the first source, stories about the prophet. In these units of tradition Elisha as a character is front and center, fashioned as the protagonist in these tales. Included here are such stories as:

- The transmission of prophetic authority to Elisha and the dividing of the Jordan (2:1-18).

- The restoration of the spring at Jericho (2:19-22).

- The punishment of the boys at Bethel (2:23-24).

- The multiplication of the widow's oil (4:1-7).

- The prophet and the Shunammite woman (4:8-37).

- Death in the pot (4:38-41).

- The feeding of the one hundred prophets at Gilgal (4:42-44).

- The recovery of the ax head from the Jordan (6:1-7).

- The miraculous power of the bones of Elisha (13:30-31).

The recurrence of themes of prophetic authority and miraculous power have been identified as commonplace in many of these individual tales. For example, Elisha's feeding of one hundred prophets at Gilgal (4:42-44) and his restoration of the spring at Jericho (2:19-22) are illustrative. In both instances Elisha wields an authority that brings about miraculous results. Another literary feature supporting the suggestion of a common source for these traditions is the narrator's point of view. In virtually all the stories of the Elisha tradition assigned to this first source the narrator's point of view evokes a very positive and laudatory assessment of the prophet. Addition-

---

[7] Most discussion concerning the history of the Elisha traditions begins with Albert Sanda's work, which identified and classified these two sources. See his *Die Bücher der Könige*. Vol. 2 (Münster in Westfalen, 1911).

ally, many of these brief episodes mention Elisha's relationship with other prophets and their very positive regard for him and dependence upon him within prophetic circles.

In fact, Elisha's congenial relationship with prophetic groups is so persistent across these narratives that it becomes the fundamental evidence leading to a proposal beyond that of source. The persistent reference to the prominent kinship between Elisha and other prophets suggests the prophetic circles themselves as the site for composition of this hypothetical source. That many of these episodes name a local shrine (Gilgal, Bethel, Jericho) where encounters between Elisha and other prophets occur suggests further not only a source but a context for the source. Prophetic circles associated with a local shrine are frequently defined as the context for the composition and development of particular tales. To summarize: literary elements such as themes, place names, point of view, and character development in the Elisha stories not only serve to suggest a source hypothesis for some of these materials; they also become the basis for proposing a context for their composition.

The source identified through literary criticism for the other materials in the Elisha stories generally is a collection of historical narratives. The events in the wider perspective of history and its unfolding constitute the main focus of interest in a historical narrative. When these kinds of materials are present in the Elisha stories, the prophet is present in the story but not necessarily at center stage. The story is an account of a historical event or development rather than being about the prophet himself. Here the accounts are not working to illustrate anything about the prophet's power or miraculous authority *per se*. Situated in the context of history, the prophet is one among several other characters. He tends not to be so much a protagonist here. His character is presented in more varied ways, and he is generally a more credible figure. The historical panorama takes priority over the individual prophet.

The collection of stories drawn from this hypothetical source includes such tales as:

- The Aramean invasion (6:8-23).

- The siege of Samaria (6:24–7:20).

- The Moabite campaign (3:4-27).

- The *coup d'état* of Hazael (8:7-15).

- The rise of Jehu (9:1-6).

It is noteworthy that the account of the siege of Samaria (6:24-33) in which the story of the cannibal mothers unfolds is among these tales. True to the literary description of this hypothetical source, Elisha's role in this tale is cursory. He is referred to once by the king when the monarch vows to behead him (6:31). Only at the conclusion of the story does he figure again, when the king's messenger, followed by the king himself, seeks out the prophet at his home (6:32-33). Consistent with the literary character of historical narrative, the siege and the famine take precedence over any spotlighting of the prophet. While he is present in the tale, Elisha is not the protagonist *per se*. Once again we see the identification and collation of literary features working to support a historical agenda, the proposal of a source, in this case a collection of historical narratives from which some of the Elisha materials were derived.

As this compositional excavation progresses, the question extends itself to sources behind the sources. In the case of our story in 2 Kings 6:24-33, investigations are conducted for the bits and pieces of tradition that contributed to the historical narratives already hypothesized. The identification of one hypothetical source leads to a speculative hunt for more hypothetical sources, moving toward hypotheses based on hypotheses. The dubious value of this enterprise becomes clear, particularly in such assessments of our text.

One scholar's literary analysis led him to conclude that two parallel sources gave rise to our story.[8] One of these sources described the siege of Samaria and an account of its citizens' starvation. In the other source a more generalized account of a widespread famine was accompanied by a brief description of the encounter between king and prophet. Other scholars were convinced that the source history of our little tale was far more complex and therefore dissected the account further.[9] Based on continuity of story line and literary integrity, they consider 6:24-33, the account of the siege of Samaria, to be part of the larger story in 6:24–7:20 that includes the resolution of the military affront as well. In the larger story, at each juncture where another character was introduced (king, prophet, gatekeeper, lepers, gatekeeper) or where the context shifted (city, prophet's house, gate, camp, city) they identified what they believed to be five self-contained units (6:24-31; 6:31-33; 7:1-2; 7:3-16; 7:17-20). These, they argued, were originally independent anecdotes derived from a fuller historical narrative. Edited together in the Elisha cycle, they eventually became the basis for prophetic biography. This analysis leads toward the conclusion that the story in 6:24-33 was composed of two of those anecdotal accounts woven into one. Thus conventional literary criticism determined that 6:24-33

---

[8] Benzinger, *Die Bücher der Könige*, 141–143.

[9] See John Gray, *I & II Kings. A Commentary* (2nd ed. Philadelphia: Westminister, 1970) 517.

is the composite of two separate units of tradition. While some argued for two parallel sources, one about Samaria and another more general story including an encounter between prophet and king, others contended that 6:24-31 and 6:31-33 were two of five originally independent anecdotes derived from one historical narrative.

One can't help but wonder about the reliability of such assessments, given the conjectural nature of virtually all the proposals. In either case the literary analysis speaks primarily to the interests of history and the possible components in the compositional history of the text. What contribution do such investigations make to the interpretation of this text? This account of just one small text is but one instance of mounting questions and objections relating to the enterprise of conventional literary criticism until its precariousness became alarmingly clear. However, dismay and dissatisfaction did not give way to despair, but to a new development in biblical studies—the emergence of a new literary criticism.

## New Literary Criticism

Around the middle of the twentieth century, scholars grew weary of the parceling and dissecting exercises that had demoted literary criticism's status to that of handmaid of history. The hunt for sources had not produced decisive conclusions. Instead, it yielded an ever-growing number of proposals. Moreover, the attention to compositional history or even the forms making up the composition (i.e., historical narrative, anecdote, saga, biographical story) had not been sufficient evidence for establishing the setting of a composition, what scholars called *Sitz im Leben*. It seemed that tracing a whole tradition along the hypothetical road of compositional accretions was as much a matter of guesswork as the source and form hypotheses on which it was grounded. Alongside the burgeoning number of proposals for the process of composition and historical context was a growing skepticism surrounding the accompanying claims and conclusions.

About the same time, literary studies in the larger academy had taken a different turn toward what was called formalist assessment of texts. These kinds of investigations were centered on the texts themselves and upgraded the status of literary texts as deserving of study on their own terms. Rather than being a means to any other ends or being dependent on historical context for their clarification, literary texts were elevated to the status of art in their own right and deemed worthy of study for their own sake. This approach to texts became known as "new literary criticism" or "new criticism." Even though it developed in the 1950s it has retained the title "new literary criticism" even today.

Under the auspices of new literary criticism the text constituted its own world and thus was justifiably an object for investigation and inquiry solely in its own autonomous aspects. No speculation about compositional past or historical setting was enlisted to determine a text's meaning. As aesthetic works, texts could be appreciated for themselves and studied by themselves. Prompted by a growing number of such projects launched in departments of literature across universities, a similar movement was soon to erupt in biblical studies as well.

In 1969 James Muilenburg delivered a presidential address titled "Form Criticism and Beyond" to the Society of Biblical Literature.[10] Educated first as a student of literature and later as a scholar of the biblical text, Muilenburg was particularly well-positioned to make this shift. He called for a move beyond historical interests, composition, sources, and even the traditional categories of form. He invited biblical scholars to entertain the interpretative possibilities that lay unattended in the artistry of the text. While Muilenburg himself and others had already begun moving in this direction within their own work, his presidential address to the biblical guild signaled the decisive turn away from dependence upon historical kinds of text excavations toward a new literary criticism in biblical studies. Hence his address served to formalize and officially commence this new direction for literary criticism that was already rapidly gaining currency in the biblical field.

Like its counterpart in departments of literature, this new literary criticism in biblical studies would not be subordinate or subservient to the goals or ends of other disciplines. It would feature the text and only the text. The literary nature of the text was to be cherished of itself. Whether a whole book like Genesis or an individual story like Jacob wrestling at the Jabbok (Gen 32:22-32), texts were now regarded as coherent, intelligible wholes, regardless of their compositional histories. They had meaning independent of compositional process, historical context, or sources of origin. Biblical interpretation had begun to emancipate itself from a dependence on what we could know from outside the text in order to account for what was in it. No longer was inquiry into the biblical writings a matter of how the text came to be written. As verbal icon, the biblical text in all its literary artistry would accommodate a new host of inquiries. Moreover, the yield from the new interpretive approach is still being harvested today.

Over the past fifty years the many different kinds of assessments conducted under the aegis of this new literary criticism have demonstrated the immense possibilities of this turn in the history of biblical interpretation. One could begin by studying the language of the text. Words of a story may

---

[10] James Muilenburg, "Form Criticism and Beyond," *JBL* 88 (1969) 1–18.

not accommodate just a single meaning but house shades of meanings, dual meanings, or even contrasting meanings. How these words are arranged—both in small units such as in phrases, clauses, and sentences, and in larger ones such as whole paragraphs, speeches, chapters, and books—is an important consideration. Grammar (the order of language) and syntax (the arrangement of language) also invited investigation.

Hence the new literary criticism summoned a close reading of how words work together to fashion a tale. The organization of a story was charted, its internal structures identified. Stylistic devices such as repetition, parallelism, and envelope patterns became foci for study. Patterns that established the outer limits of a story world were mapped. Artistic organization of individual small and large units of tradition as well as how various literary strategies wove the units together came under assessment.

This new literary criticism also invited the kinds of investigation that would appreciate the biblical writings specifically as narrative literature. These included the larger questions about character development, the elements of plot, and matters of tone. Features such as narrative speed, how tension is introduced into the story line, and how it is resolved became significant. Also worthy of attention was the introduction of direct discourse or the patterns of direct speech between characters. The fashioning of dialogue itself along with small and large movements in dialogue merited appraisal.

As such avenues of literary study continued to increase, another point of inquiry became how the work achieves its specific effect upon its audience. What is the mood of a story? What emotion does this mood cultivate, or what response does it provoke? Is the writing stylized to persuade, to instruct, or to entertain? All these inquiries led one to a fuller appreciation of the text and its potential for meaning.

Point of view can also be a very instructive lens in consideration of both the text and the text's effect upon an intended audience. The point of view of the narrator or of an individual character can be taken up. Whether the narrator is impartial to the various characters or sympathetic to some and not to others reveals a great deal about the story. Examining point of view in a tale can also inform us how the would-be reader is being coaxed into a particular perspective on the events in a story or on an individual character. Readers may be afforded information that some of the characters don't have. They may be awarded a vantage point in the story line that sets them at odds with some or all of the characters. Such compositional strategies encourage the reader's identification with some individuals in a tale and dissociate the reader from others.

As the possibilities for study under this new literary criticism continue to grow, an underlying assumption about the biblical text as literature becomes more and more pronounced. The text as autonomous whole is paramount. In its revelatory capacity, the text invites our gaze upon it alone. While the new literary criticism does not deny that there were many and complex stages involved in the text's composition, this kind of literary assessment is fixed upon only the final form of the text. New literary criticism rivets its attention upon the text. Like a novice standing before a great painting, new literary criticism tries to behold the artistic and cooperative interplay between content and form and the meaning disclosed therein.

Still, this is not passive gazing at a work of art. Rather, one works to grasp the intricacy of sentences, to consider the choice and location of words, to discern the design of a plot, and to study the characteristic features of its narrative. Only then can the integrity of the story world begin to emerge and its depth of meaning begin to be known.

Our own story of the cannibal mothers lends itself readily to this new form of literary assessment. It proves its status as a literary artifact, rich and abundant with possibilities for meaning. Every word seems to invite attention for its location, design, and interpretive potential in the larger tale. Even the formulaic words at the beginning and ending of the story disclose purpose.

The account opens with "Some time later . . . ." Subtly these opening words convey that what follows is later than but related to what just preceded. As the tale begins, its opening words draw attention to and suggest some connection or symmetry with the prior episode. In the preceding tale (6:8-23) Israel had been successful in defeating the Arameans. However, on Elisha's advice the enemies were set free to return home. In a reversal of circumstances, in our tale the Arameans now lay siege to Samaria, the capital in Israel (6:24–7:20). In the first tale Israel seizes the Aramean army. In the second, the Aramean army surrounds Israel's capital, Samaria. Though juxtaposed side by side, the stories in 6:8-23 and 6:24–7:20 tell opposing tales.

6:8-23 Israel's siege on the Arameans ⬅➡ 6.24–7:20 Aramean siege on Israel

Yet the stories are linked. In the second story, our story, the king holds the prophet responsible for the siege (v. 31). That the king blames the prophet for this desperate situation in Samaria (v. 31) can only be understood in light of the previous story. It was the prophet's advice that the Aramean army be set free that makes him subject to blame for this new attack. This opposition prepares for the conflict between king and prophet, the centerpiece of our story. And it is this conflict between king and prophet that determines the course of our story and invites resolution.

As our story in 6:24-33 begins, it also connects with what follows in that it constitutes one of two episodes in the larger drama of the siege of Samaria and its resolution. In literary terms an "episode" can be defined as an incident that stands out by itself with its own plot but is connected to the plot of a larger series of events.[11] In our case the episodes in 6:24-33 and 7:1-20 are integrally woven together. The resolution of the crisis between king and prophet in 6:24-33 prompts the resolution of the crisis of the Aramean siege of Israel at Samaria (7:1-20).

Literary assessments typically identify three elements in the development of plot: *exposition, climax,* and *resolution.* In the *exposition* such matters as time, place, and background of the story are established. Characters might be introduced and relevant information provided. In the course of this stage setting the story's complicating problem is introduced. In our story 6:24-30 offers an opening exposition. We hear that Aram has mustered its whole army and laid siege to the Israelite capital of Samaria. In turn the disastrous circumstances for all those who live there are detailed. The siege has had devastating effects upon the people's economic well-being. In the marketplace the least palatable of goods are exorbitantly priced. This general state of economic crisis has wrought catastrophic consequences in the lives of individual citizens. Now the narrative camera momentarily zooms in on a woman and her circumstances to further dramatize the problem. She tells her story of an agreement with another woman to eat their children. However, the crisis of cannibalism is compounded with an even further problem. The two have boiled and eaten this woman's child the day before. Now the other woman has refused to surrender her child. The crisis of the nation has created a crisis for these two individual citizens. The narrative move from the general description of the siege (vv. 24-25) to the particular circumstances of the starving women (vv. 26-31) allows us to grasp the grave effects of the larger national circumstances on the individual lives of the inhabitants of Samaria.

Additionally, the severity of the crisis serves to anticipate and intensify the conflict between king and prophet. Had Elijah not ordered the release of the Aramean army there would be no siege. In the absence of a siege the economy would be flourishing. Citizens would not be starving; nor would they be eating their children. At first glance the prophet appears at fault. The king's vow, which concludes this long exposition, makes explicit the conflict at the heart of our tale. "So may God do to me, and more, if the head of Elisha son of Shaphat stays on his shoulders today" (v. 31).

---

[11] Clarence L. Barnhart, ed., *The New Century Handbook of English Literature* (New York: Appleton-Century Crofts, 1967) 403–404.

The conflict between king and prophet constitutes the problem emanating from the exposition.

As the king's messenger hurries to Elisha's house, presumably to fulfill the royal vow to decapitate the prophet, the story hurries to a *climax*. The *climax* marks the point of highest dramatic tension in a tale. It is the turning point in a story and determines how the problem will be resolved. The setting of our narrative now shifts to Elisha's location, the destination of the royal assassin. We are told that Elisha is sitting in his house along with some elders and anticipates the arrival of the king's hatchet man. The approaching assault warrants a defensive gesture. Elisha orders that his doors be bolted shut. Narrative tension mounts as the prophet's posture of self-defense counters the approach of the prophet's potential executioner.

*Resolution* is the third and final element in a plot's construction. It ends impasses, solves conflicts, determines winners, and brings stories to a close. The *resolution* in our tale is as unexpected as it is brief. In an abrupt and unexplained shift in the narrative we now hear that the king himself is *en route* to the prophet's house. When he arrives the crisis is resolved, not by the anticipated violent brawl but by the king's confession before the prophet of his powerlessness and despair. Concluding that God is in charge of the current circumstances, he says, "This trouble is from the LORD! Why should I hope in the LORD any longer?" (v. 33). His majesty's statement of helplessness and hopelessness before the prophet overturns and replaces his animosity toward Elisha. With the king's change of heart their conflict reaches resolution.

As the story unfolds, meaning is disclosed in a wealth of contrasts and parallels. First two sets of parallels spotlight the two key players, the king and then the prophet. In the first part of the story our attention is twice directed to the king walking on the wall (vv. 26, 31). Elevated above the fray of the dire economic conditions, the king paces atop the wall surrounding the city. In the later part of the tale the narrative twice notes the sitting posture of first Elisha and then the elders in his house (v. 32). Sitting in his house confined within the city, Elisha too is subject to the conditions of the siege like the rest of the people.

> Now as *the king of Israel was walking on the city wall* . . . (v. 26)
> now since *he* [the king] *was walking on the city wall* . . . (v. 31)
>
> Now *Elisha was sitting* in his house (v. 32)
> and the elders were *sitting with him* [Elisha]. (v. 32)

Out of these parallels arise opposition. The twice-mentioned reference to the king "walking" atop the city wall contrasts with the twice-mentioned participle "sitting" in the description of the prophet and elders gathered in his house (v. 32). Here the artistic formulation of contrast between king and prophet serves to reinforce their conflict as the heart of the story.

The difference in location between these two parties hints at their social difference in relation to the people. The king is elevated above the starving citizens below. By contrast, the prophet sits in his house among some of the people's elders. The king's nervous and solitary pacing, above the citizens and removed from them, contrasts with the prophet's calm position at home among others in his house. The description of the prophet's unruffled demeanor suggests a confidence and authority that the all-powerful king seems to lack. It may be this quiet authority on the part of Elisha that soon prompts a change of heart on the part of the monarch. Though bent upon beheading the prophet he holds responsible for the current circumstances, the king has an abrupt change of heart when he arrives at the prophet's house. Instead of demanding the prophet's life the king confesses his own desperation and despair.

That confession of despair at the close of this episode reminds us of the king's response to the starving woman's request for help at the opening of the tale.

> "No! Let the LORD help you. How can I help you? From the threshing floor or from the wine press?" (v. 27)

> "This trouble is from the LORD. Why should I hope in the LORD any longer?" (v. 33)

Confronted by the woman's plea for help, the king testifies to his own helplessness (v. 27). When encountering the prophet at his house, once again the king expresses despair (v. 33). In both instances the LORD's inaction is at the root of his antipathy.

The king's confession before the prophet diffuses the conflict between these two parties. The twice-told despondency on the part of the monarch warrants the prophet's intervention. The king's confession of pessimism concludes the tale, forming a sharp contrast with the opening of the following story, where Elisha makes a proclamation of optimism. In 7:1 the prophet announces the end of the siege and the famine. A desperate group of lepers will be the instruments who realize the prophet's word in the tale that follows. Hence the contrast between the monarch's impotence and the prophet's prowess in our episode is further magnified by the contrasts that erupt in the following tale.

Throughout our story we encounter the impotence of a powerful ruler who can end neither the siege nor the resulting famine. In the story that follows we watch a group of desperate, powerless lepers whose discovery of the deserted Aramean camp and actions in informing the king of the enemy's departure bring an end to the siege and the famine. Overshadowed by the prophet in word and surpassed by the lepers in deed, the king limps along as the main character in the narrative. Still, in keeping with the new criticism's focus on building blocks of the story world, this pathetic king remains the focal point of attention and evaluation. As we keep our gaze fixed upon the artistic strategy and integrity of the story, the conflict between king and prophet assumes center stage. It is the axis around which the rest of the story rotates and the connection on which the next episode hinges. Though the resolution of the conflict favors the prophet, the contrasting character of the king is an essential instrument for making that disclosure.

King and prophet, prophet and king—the narrative description above has riveted our attention on them and made them the key players of the story. Stylistics of parallels and contrasts work to reinforce their opposition. Their conflict builds narrative tension that creates the climax. The resolution of the plot hinges on the resolution of their conflict. Plot, stylistics, characterization—all work in favor of highlighting the central and governing role of king and prophet in the narrative outcome. There can be no dispute that in the conventional categories of literary criticism these are the central and controlling characters.

In these kinds of assessments, where unity and integrity of story are paramount, the story of the cannibal mothers is background. Their tale is never completed. How the mothers' crisis is addressed, or if it is ever addressed, never surfaces in the tale. Rather, the mothers' story functions as mere literary prop. It draws attention to the king by highlighting his helplessness before starving citizens. It serves as an illustration of the gravity of the famine. It provides a motive for the king's animosity toward the prophet. It creates urgency, prompting the prophet's reversal of the circumstances of famine. Though instrumental in crafting the conflict between king and prophet, still the mothers' tale is peripheral to the larger story. The interest on the part of new literary criticism in literary features for their own sake holds the king and prophet at center stage.

When compared to conventional literary study, new literary criticism is emancipatory. It frees the text from the objectives and interests of historical studies. It unveils meaning in the text as an autonomous entity. It reads forms such as parallel language, repetitions, envelope patterns in concert with content, the story line. Form and content work together as partners in the production of meaning. Such a focus leads to appreciation of the immense artistry that crafts and animates a tale. On the other hand, new literary criticism is also shortsighted. It fails to recognize that the artistry in a text like the story in 6:24-33, which appears to spotlight the king and prophet, is first and foremost "in the eye of the beholder." What one sees in the text has a lot to do with who is doing the "seeing." Our own experience, culture, and commitments train our eye upon what is art, who is important, and what is significant in a text.

Moreover, literary reading founded upon unity or a reading that seeks coherence in a tale has to ignore what is missing in stories. Seams, gaps, and silences abound in the biblical stories, and these can be as revelatory as what is present in a tale. In addition, characters in the background can be as informative as those who are front and center stage. Those who do not have the power of speech tell something about those who do. A literary criticism that privileges only those stories that get completed or those characters that are the protagonists or main characters according to the traditional assessment may be as shortsighted as a society that does the same. Moreover, a literary criticism that reads and investigates for wholeness, unity, and integrity in texts offers interpretations that tell only half the story.

## Postmodern Literary Criticism

A charged notion, the term "postmodern" rarely evokes neutral responses. Its use either enkindles an applause of allegiance or sets off a staunch march of dissent. It is messy in the way it accommodates a myriad of associations and harrowing in the way it overturns modernist assumptions. As an intellectual posture the postmodern does not lend itself to easy or singular definition. In fact, given that postmodernism rejects totalizing systems of meaning—that something means this and only this—any one definition of "postmodern" should be viewed as suspect.

François Lyotard, a French philosopher, first gave currency to the term "postmodernism." He defined it with the now familiar expression "incredulity toward metanarratives."[12] Responding to his own circumstances in France during the Second World War, Lyotard's critique of modernity was initially directed toward political, economic, and social systems claiming to be "foundational." For Lyotard the reigning cultural paradigms that define society, social systems, and theories constituted the metanarratives. Marxism, empiricism, rationalism, and capitalism numbered among them. According to Lyotard these systems are grand stories or narratives claiming to disclose the meaning of all other stories. They have oriented research, fixed

---

[12] François Lyotard, *The Postmodern Condition*, translated by Geoff Fennington and Brian Massumi. Theory and History of Literature 10 (Minneapolis: University of Minnesota Press, 1984).

results, determined behavior, and defined what is "truth." That they claim to speak for the many earns them their status as metanarratives.

The incredulity that Lyotard talks about stems from the realization that these "big stories" have deceived us. They have made promises they could not keep. They set themselves up as templates that in the end don't orient history or define human destiny as promised. When they are set against the events of this century their inherent fallacies are disclosed. In one of his works Lyotard cites Auschwitz as one chilling instance that reveals this deception.[13]

Prompted by Lyotard's critique, the ongoing examination of the credibility of claims to truth did not remain confined to the political, social, and economic systems that order and define society. Scrutiny extends now to the philosophical foundations upon which these systems are founded as well as the foundations of academic disciplines beyond political science and economics. Literary criticism and its approaches to interpretation number among these systems up for assessment. Literary criticism along with other academic ventures that produce meaning, navigating human existence or inscribing life with meaning, come under intense scrutiny. Working assumptions and methods of interpretation that produce meaning on the way to truth claims are subject to the postmodern critique. The consequences of postmodernism for interpretation itself, as well as the methods designed to arrive at interpretation, have become clear. Meaning enshrined as foundational or meaning generated as support for truth claims now must be viewed with suspicion or even rejected outright.

Postmodernism's influence, though disruptive, was not abrupt. In biblical studies the stable foundation of meaning on which interpretation is founded—whether that of compositional history (conventional literary criticism) or literary artistry (new literary criticism)—had already shown its shortcomings over a period of some fifty years. In light of these deficits postmodernism sets in relief a question increasingly on the minds of biblical critics. Can any method or system achieve ultimate clarity or credibility in regard to meaning—whether of a text or of any aspect of life? In response postmodernism proposes that all meaning is constructed and therefore contingent. On such grounds no meaning can be foundational or, for that matter, universal. Hence postmodernism characteristically rejects claims to universality and completeness while also rejecting claims of privilege or supremacy of any approach to interpretation. Methods themselves are made up or constructed and thus also destabilized as guarantors of meaning.

---

[13] Ibid. 59.

In terms of literary studies this does not mean that methods no longer qualify as viable or defensible ways to study texts. Rather, when postmodernism modifies literary studies it invites us to read and interpret texts in a way that accommodates a multiplicity of approaches. Moreover, since approaches are as much constructed as the texts themselves, postmodernism would urge us to enlist a whole cadre of interpretive angles—not just those that endorse the views of the text, but also approaches that critique and challenge the text.

What, then, does postmodern literary criticism look like? Less a method and more a mindset, postmodern literary criticism includes a variety of working assumptions about texts and literary studies that increasingly characterize the practices of a new generation of critics.[14] Since some of them will be particularly relevant to our literary analysis of the two cannibal mothers before the king, these assumptions will be discussed here. These include: understanding literary texts as discourse, viewing texts in materialistic terms, recognizing the reader's role in interpretation, and fostering a heightened interest in the fragmentary, contradictory, and contentious elements in texts.

## *Literary Texts as Discourse*

The impact of Michel Foucault and his work has been profound in the shaping of postmodern thought. Following Foucault's influential usage, literature has been cast as discourse. As such, literary texts are viewed as a process rather than a product or as someone's production. As process a text is understood as exceedingly social, enmeshed with the institutions and mechanisms that author, mediate, and control the flow of knowledge and power in a community. However, literature as discourse is not alone. Intellectual theories, political debates, even television commercials are among its many companions. Everything is discourse. Moreover, discourse refers not just to the content of the writing, whether that be the story line of a narrative, the tenets of a political debate, or the arguments of a philosophical treatise. Discourse also includes the myriad ways such discussions, their representations, and their productions are ensnared in the mundane conditions of people's lives.

---

[14] For an introduction to postmodern biblical criticism see The Bible and Culture Collective, *The Postmodern Bible* (New Haven: Yale University Press, 1995); A.K.M. Adam, ed., *Handbook of Postmodern Biblical Interpretation.* 2 vols. (St. Louis: Chalice, 2000); A.K.M. Adam, *What Is Postmodern Biblical Criticism?* (Minneapolis: Fortress, 1995).

For example, a book providing a commentary on the biblical book of Hosea narrates not only important information on this Israelite prophet, his message, and its implications for today. That same commentary also discloses information about the academic and publishing worlds. It represents the academic trends in text interpretations and it reveals who has the power to "author" such work. It also shows what kind of information on a prophet will make for a marketable book as well as offering some insight into what gets published and who gets published.

To study texts as discourse is to study them for how they reveal and participate in these domains of power and knowledge. The biblical traditions themselves are acts of engagement with a vast and diverse reality. They are made up of different and even opposing beliefs, values, biases, and investments. Like all texts, they are caught up in the complex and contestatory processes by which a society defines and maintains its organizations and institutions, even its self-understanding. Societies are continuously caught up in the struggles whereby one segment of culture defines itself as dominant over and against a subservient segment defined as "the other." The construction of discourses bears an imprint of these differences. Hence discourse analysis discloses these contestatory processes at work in the writing itself. It might reveal how a story participates in a class struggle or whom a text supports in the struggle or whom it might undercut in the interests of class relations. Discourse analysis might also unveil the support for powerful figures or institutions in a society or revolt against such figures and institutions. Consequently, when literary criticism engages in discourse analysis, literature reveals much more than the intrinsic artistry of a story. It can provide evidence of the social and political entanglements of the society that produced the literature and also of the subsequent communities that received it.

Our story of the cannibal mothers invites such inquiry. Is the conflict between mothers related to the conflict between king and prophet? Why are mothers eating their children used to show how serious the famine has become? Why even include their story when we never hear the outcome? What does their being in the story reveal about their relations to institutions of power? Is rivalry between women in any way related to the maintenance of hierarchical structures?

## Viewing Texts in Materialist Terms

Characterizing literary texts as discourse highlights their enmeshment in a social and cultural matrix. They exist within the political and economic dynamics of production of the text and readership. They are not timeless entities, as new literary criticism presumes, but, like other objects in culture, they belong to a material reality. The term "material" here refers to goods within a context. It takes into account the production and distribution of goods and the related issues of power and its circulation. It considers the social relations between owners and workers, and differences in social classes that are involved in their composition or repression.

Viewing literary texts in materialist terms positions them on equal footing with other social and cultural practices, artifacts, relics, and remnants of a past. Like displays we might see in a gallery or museum, literary texts stand alongside other material evidence. One can take the stance of an anthropologist to look at how these vestiges of the past taken together craft a social context. Instead of being viewed against a constructed social backdrop, literary texts are part of the construction. Of interest here is *how,* not what forces (historical, social, economic, biographical, sexual, aesthetic, psychological, etc.) interact with these productions and interpretive practices.

This enlistment of literature such as the Bible with other cultural phenomena in the makeup of context changes our understanding of literature. Distinctions such as foreground/background are no longer accurate or adequate categories if we wish to understand literature in relation to social or historical contexts. Instead, a biblical story and its social context are thought to reside in a dynamic relationship in which they mutually shape and define one another. Postmodern literary criticism is interested in this mutual fashioning. How does a biblical story help in the construction of a social context, and how does the social context shape the production of that tale? This dynamic commands interest.

When we become aware of the shaping power of discourse we consider texts for signs of their social and political impact as well as for imprints of the social and political forces on the text. Attending to these relations, we study texts to see how they articulate hierarchies of value, power, and meaning. Any powerful institution necessarily controls the very meaning of the discourse used to discuss it. A materialist reading explores the relationship between power and language, between discourse and politics. It seeks to hear the voices excluded from the writing, attending to traces of those who do not take part in the narratives of power.

Whether texts are intended as entertaining, instructive, or confessional, they are, at the same time, social productions. As material evidence of production and reception they function not so much as windows but as representations. Directly or indirectly they represent what is important, the configurations of social class and the patterns of relations that define a society. Whether they are biblical stories, law codes, novels, or annals of royalty, texts constitute a record of practices by which a social group organizes its meaning and values. The texts might disclose how the group is organized, what its sites of power are, and what kind of power they exhibit. The struggles, conflicts, and identifications between groups might also be revealed. On whose behalf the texts speak, what groups they highlight, and which ones they relegate to the background can be disclosed. In short, postmodern literary criticism takes texts into account as material evidence to study how discourse functions socially and on whose behalf.

In our story, does the struggle between king and prophet indicate where the primary sites of power are for that society? Does the representation of the women in the story suggest something about their status? Is it significant that the conflict between king and prophet governs the story rather than the conflict between the women? Additionally, does the practice of cannibalism indicate anything about the value system of the society producing this tale? What are the configurations of social relations in which women would agree to eat their children?

## *Recognition of the Reader's Role in Interpretation*

Of all the contributing factors prompting the postmodernist turn, perhaps none is more influential than the attention to the reader. Modern approaches to reading texts had emphasized the background of a story or the form and content of the writing itself. Meaning was something encased in the text that could be discovered and extracted with the right "tools." The objectivity of the text and the objectivity of methods were considered to guarantee the objectivity of the results.

Out of all this fixation on the text as object evolved a fascination with what was first identified as "the implied reader." Formalist studies practiced "closed readings," that is, attention was limited to what was inside the covers of the book. As they scoured the text for every kind of internal feature they began to identify elements of both style and content indicative of the reader for whom the writing was intended. The construction of that portrait was called "the implied reader," and it corroborated historical studies and its interests. While confidence in retrieving the author's intended meaning had waned, the prospect of determining the reader or audience for whom the work was written only resuscitated historians' interest in authorial intention. However, now *what* the author intended was to be replaced by *who* the author intended as his or her reader. For a time reader-response criticism appeared as a new stronghold. It featured the detection of an implied reader by means of close readings according to the precepts of new literary criticism. At the same time it satisfied conventional literary criticism's interest in matters of composition and authorial intention. However, as it turns out, reader-response criticism was the last bastion for both conventional literary criticism and new literary criticism. What became glaringly apparent was that it takes a real reader to discern the existence and character of an implied reader. Moreover, the implied reader and the real reader do not enjoy independent status. The growing attention to issues of power and knowledge disclosed that the implied reader is more like the real reader.[15]

Acknowledgment of the reader's role had shattering implications for some of the most central assumptions in literary interpretation. The objectivity of texts and methods was no longer defensible. The intentions of the hypothetical reader were perilously identical with the real reader/interpreter's intention. Hence interpretations long defended as grounded in empirical evidence and objective data turned out to be glaringly contingent upon that real reader.

Now the readers and their influence became as much the focus as the text itself. The background of the reader along with the background of the text became the formative, and at times formidable elements in interpretations. What are a reader's experiences, values, history, and culture? The impact of these elements on readers' perspectives and strategies became part of investigative focus. For example, in Judges 20–21 the Israelite tribes pledge themselves to avenge a horrific crime committed by their brother tribe Benjamin. As the story unfolds the tribe of Benjamin is annihilated and its people flee, taking refuge in forests. Whole villages of men and women are slain. Maidens are carried off by warriors. The complex issues prompting and comprising this military confrontation between tribes provoke more than one response from readers. One reader's experience may condition him or her to see only just retribution and bravery in the war story of the Israelites' victory over the wayward Benjaminites. However, another reader's experience may prompt him or her to behold only senseless bloodshed and the victimization of women in the same tale. Gradually we begin to see how subjective, political, and biased interpretation really is. At the same time we may also begin to grasp that what constitutes the story in the text is itself conditioned by the reader.

Women, ethnic minorities, and Third World readers have been especially instrumental in forging this new focus. Their readings of the biblical texts transgress the decorum and longstanding traditions of reigning modes of interpretation. Not only have they exposed the role of the reader in

---

[15] Jane Tompkins has edited a series of essays that overview the theoretical positions developed under the aegis of reader response criticism. These include the mock reader, narratee, super reader, passive reader, implied reader, informed reader, ideal reader, leading up to the real reader. See Jane P. Tompkins, ed., *Reader-Response Criticism: From Formalism to Post-Structuralism* (Baltimore: Johns Hopkins University Press, 1980).

interpretation; more importantly, they have exposed the role that power and privilege play in this process. Significantly, too, their experiences and histories, when brought to bear on these texts that are sacred to Jews and Christians, have raised serious concerns about the truth claims critics make for what they do with these writings and how they do it. Hence these once-marginalized voices have revealed just how socially and politically contingent interpretive practices are. In addition, they have uncovered not only the contingency of the practices but of interpretations themselves. For example, how one interprets the story of Israel's exodus from Egyptian bondage and subsequent settlement in the land has a lot to do with where the reader is situated in culture and history. If one is an early Christian escaping from the persecuting enemy or more recently a Latin American reader awaiting release from political oppressors one is apt to focus on the Israelites' release from bondage. On the other hand, if the reader is thoughtlessly conditioned by anti-Jewish sentiments or if one is a Native American whose tribal land rights were unjustly confiscated centuries ago one might center one's interpretive attention on the horrific fate of the Canaanites who, according to the biblical story, were the original inhabitants of the land.

Meaning once thought to be encased in the text now shows itself to be caught up and intertwined with the experience of the reader. Interpretation once thought to be wedded to historical context shows itself to be dependent upon the social location and political commitments of a reader. Without a doubt, moving to the forefront are questions of who has the power to interpret, whose interpretation counts, and what is deemed as the essential knowledge for the process of interpretation. With issues of power and knowledge at stake, literary criticism locks arms with discourse analysis. Hence postmodern literary criticism is concerned not only with the socio-political process in the production of a text but also with the socio-political process in the reception of that text.

This fascination with the role of readers and their experiences in interpreting the text has become one of the hallmarks of postmodern interpretation. But readers are plural. Hence postmodern literary criticism necessarily urges and accommodates readerly perspectives that are eclectic, variegated, and multi-voiced. Granted, this does make for a less tidy arena of interpretations surrounding a text. However, the diversity of readers and readings spanning a text's interpretive history insures against the reign of any one interpretation and the socio-political commitments latent therein. For example, in our story of the cannibal mothers, readers can read in a manner that spotlights the king and the prophet or can resist that identification. Readers whose life experience included teetering on the brink of violent annihilation may read the story with a fixation upon the situation between the two women while ignoring the dispute between the king and the prophet. Feminist readers of this text may ignore the prophet and king and read this story *in memoriam* of these women and children.

## Interest in the Fragmentary, Contradictory, and Contestatory Elements in Texts

Both conventional literary criticism and new literary criticism are grounded in a common assumption about texts. Conventional literary criticism traces the stages of composition that lead to a text's literary wholeness and completion. New literary criticism begins with the assumption of a text's wholeness and unity and reads the poetics crafting this achievement. Hence both conventional literary criticism and new literary criticism take for granted an underlying integrity and wholeness in a story. Moreover, the classification of the biblical writings as "literature" explains such ascriptions, because these are the attributes we presume of literature. We assign it an autonomy, an aesthetic quality, and an integrity that separates it from the mundane or from other more ordinary kinds of writings. It claims a membership in that domain called culture that is spelled with a capital "C."

Postmodern literary criticism takes issue with the very category "literature." It argues that all texts—whether they are phone books, legal treatises, novels, religious prayer books, or what we call literature—are constituted by and constituting of social life, social processes, and social hierarchies. Postmodern criticism rejects distinctions between the aesthetic and material realms and views them as mutually fashioning of each other. A play can be constructed by the social mores of a particular group in a society. At the same time that play can reinforce the social configuration that gives that particular group its elite status and its social power.

Additionally, while postmodern literary criticism recognizes the literary forms, stylistics, and poetics employed in compositions, it takes issue with the sole pursuit of unity and literary integrity of a writing as if these were something organic to the text. Rather, it argues that such configurations are not necessarily embedded in literature but are the results of selective investigation. For example, in our story according to the habits of new literary criticism, readings have noted how the poetics of parallelism juxtapose the king and the prophet in opposition to one another. As we have seen, the artistic formulation of contrast between king and prophet reinforces their conflict, making it the heart of the story.

> Now as *the king of Israel was walking on the city wall* . . . (v. 26)
> now since *he* [the king] *was walking on the city wall* . . . (v. 32)

Now *Elisha was sitting* in his house (v. 32)
and the elders were *sitting with him* [Elisha]. (v. 32)

This juxtaposition of the king and prophet in different positions and different locations coincides with the differences that lead to conflict between them.

However, other takes on the literary arrangement of the tale might resist this outcome and argue literary integrity in other terms. For example, the postmodern reading that follows discloses a different literary organization.

v. 24 Ben-Hadad and his army

                           Authorities in a struggle for power

  v. 26 Israel's king walking on the
      wall of the city

    vv. 27-29 Woman and her story    Mothers in a struggle for a child's
                                        life as food

  v. 30 Israel's king walking on the
      wall of the city

                           Authorities in a struggle for power

vv. 31-33 Prophet and elders

Here conflict reigns across the narrative, but the women's conflict is the centerpiece of the tale. While the artistic organization proposed in the first instance features the conflict between king and prophet, the artistic arrangement proposed in the second puts the women's dispute at center stage. However, postmodern interpretation is less interested in arguing one arrangement over another and more interested in arguing that literary integrity and organization are not something organic or intrinsic to the text.

Moreover, the very pursuit of literary organization, unity, and integrity ignores the accompanying gaps, contradictions, seams, or disjunctions in a work. Convinced that "whole readings" are, at times, only a self-satisfying illusion, postmodern literary criticism opts for more fragmentary kinds of considerations. Resisting the tendency to integrate dominant images, dialogues, and characters into a single master discourse, it attends to fleeting references, incongruities, or unanswered questions resident at the borders or in the margins of the text.

For example, in 2 Kings 22–23 the story of King Josiah's religious reform unfolds. This well-regarded ruler of the nation of Judah is conducting a massive religious reform instigated by the discovery of a law book during the Temple renovation. He orders all the local shrines closed, the houses of sacred prostitution boarded up, and puts off limits all the altars to the sun, moon, and stars and the sacrifices conducted there. If we follow the story line in the company of most critics we enter a debate as to whether the monarch's action was prompted by religious fervor or political savvy. Centralization of cult or the requirement that all religious worship be conducted in the capital, Jerusalem, could be an expression of conversion and a commitment to turn the whole nation in its religious practices away from foreign deities and toward worship of YHWH alone. On the other hand, centralization of cult in Jerusalem would also centralize all the allegiance and monies that supported the elaborate cultic practices in the towns and villages, thus strengthening the king's governance.

However, postmodern literary criticism reads otherwise. With the centralization of cult in one city, Jerusalem, it would ask about the plight of the women who once worked at cultic shrines in and around Jerusalem and were now unemployed in that urban center because of this king's reform. At the same time it would consider the disruption of village life and the threatened economics of peasants' livelihood resulting from the dismantling of local shrines in the villages far from the capital. It would acknowledge the impact of religious gesture on the promotion of nationalism and the influence of nationalism on the formation of religious actions. Perhaps it would end with questions rather than conclusions—questions about the nature of religious reform and programs of renewal; what prompts such programs of renewal, reform, or centralization? Who benefits from these changes? What are the relations of the beneficiaries to the reigning political paradigm? Do such programs change hearts, or do they change economics? Instead of being captivated by literary details of this king's centralization of cult, a postmodern literary criticism would inquire about how hierarchical forms of power become the enabling conditions of such detailed representations. For example, what are the forces at work in our tale and in the history of interpretation that include a story about the cannibal mothers in a story about the king and the prophet? Why is the women's story left without a resolution? What does this lack of conclusion to their plight reveal about the reigning political paradigm?

As the fulcrum of postmodern literary studies shifts from that of previous kinds of approaches it yields different outcomes. It often features ambiguity rather than airtight arguments. It struggles with chaos rather than selectively sketching coherence. It attends to the polyphony of voices in contest rather than assenting to a monologue of one dominant discourse, and in the end it discloses complexity and provokes inquiry rather than promoting the pretense of closure.

As postmodern literary criticism pays attention to the seams, unanswered questions, or cracks in the narrative it often uncovers competing voices, values, and centers of power in the story. It raises unaddressed questions lurking in the margins that disrupt the integrity of a unified reading. Attention to these contradictory, contestatory, or incongruous elements in texts often leads to interpretations that challenge the prevailing wisdom about a biblical story. In the process we discover how rhetoric is not just artistic or innocent but may participate in the violence of exclusion. We discover that parallelisms or repetitions are not just benign literary devices but may work to set borders of exclusion and marginalization. We may be surprised that the casting of one character as major and central to a story-line has the grave consequence of demoting others or reinforcing their marginalized status as represented in a text and in the society that produces it. On such grounds, postmodern literary analysis becomes an appropriate and essential lens by which to conduct a character study of minor characters. In the chapters that follow, a postmodern literary analysis will offer an assessment of our tale on behalf of the two cannibal mothers. In the process these "minor characters," often overlooked in the story and misjudged in the history of interpretation, may have a "major" contribution to make in the building up of our own character.

PART II

# CHAPTER FOUR

## A Postmodern Literary Study
## of Two Cannibal Mothers Before a King
## (2 Kings 6:24-33)[1]

This chapter's study of the two cannibal mothers before a king levels a challenge to the received wisdom about this tale, a wisdom that honors a prophet and assesses a king while ignoring or condemning the desperate situation of two women and their children. At the same time, a postmodern literary study of these minor characters has other unexpected outcomes. It exposes the cost incurred for paying attention only to major characters and living by those interpretations. It exposes the subtle but nevertheless real violence seeded by ignoring the so-called "insignificant characters" such as the women in this tale. Moreover, it considers the mimetic kinship between interpretations that look away from these mothers and their plight, and the practices and social mores of a society that promote such interpretations.

More than idle curiosity prompts such a study. Rather, it is based on a belief that how we study and interpret texts matters, and that the study of such formative and influential literature as the Bible matters even more. Along these lines, then, a postmodern literary assessment of the two canni- bal mothers hopes to do more than generate a study of a minor character. It also intends to provoke a dialogue about violence—a violence that results from the privileging of the powerful and the empowering of the privi- leged—both in texts and in society. Such exchanges and their consequences are not confined to any time period or context, but crisscross and rebound

[1] An earlier version of this chapter appeared as an article entitled "Forms of Violence and the Violence of Forms: Two Cannibal Mothers Before a King (2 Kings 6:24-33)" in *Journal of Feminist Studies in Religion* 14 (1998) 91–104.

between individuals and whole populations and between ancient and contemporary culture. These interpretations about texts and violence are not just about the ancient world of the Bible. They are also about us. Forms of violence erupting from the circulation of power and privilege corroborate and exacerbate further violence, a violence of forms: in this instance the form of a biblical story about two cannibal mothers and the form of its interpretations.

As we have already noted, the story told in 2 Kings 6:24-33 resides within the larger literary unit of 2 Kings 6:8–7:20, which in turn belongs to the surrounding Elisha narrative complex. Though our story bears kinship with the surrounding literary framework, the content of the tale confines the story and its characters within the walls of a city. It opens by reporting with unspecified historical references that Ben-Hadad, an Aramean king, and his Syrian forces have besieged Samaria and surrounded the city. These grave political conditions on the national level have wrought even more serious circumstances on the economic and domestic front. A sample of market prices for undesirable goods confirms this. Then a horrific disclosure on the part of a mother seeking the king's help further dramatizes this crisis for individual citizens. The king blames the prophet. At this point the story turns and fixes on the controversy between these two officials. It is as if all that has preceded in this account was in the interest of leading up to this focal moment. The resolution of the problem comes quickly when the king, bent upon beheading the prophet, has an unexplained change of heart. Arriving at the door of the prophet's house, the king confesses his despair and lack of faith in God.

Where the story ends, interpretation begins—with a focus on the king and the prophet. Down through the ages prophet and king, king and prophet have focalized all attention and all interpretation. Some studies fix on the "why" of their opposition. The dire conditions caused by the famine might have occasioned their controversy. The prophet's insistence that the Syrian army be let go might explain the king's animosity toward this man of God. Additionally, the power and influence that both king and prophet wield in the society necessarily make them frequent opponents.

Across interpretive discussions the prophet is most often considered the one "in the right." After all, this *is* a biblical story and the prophet *is* considered to be God's intermediary. And in the story the prophet's authority does overshadow the king's hostility, and the famine does end the following day. But let's also keep in mind that prophets are no more flawless characters than are kings. And let's keep an open mind that allows us to see disjunctions or seams in the construction of this biblical personage, the prophet. Even this "man of God" has struggles—and maybe a dark side as well.

By contrast, the king is an easy target for blame. His crooked edges and shortcomings are much more visible and thus easy to fix upon. In the opening of the story he blames God for the crisis of food shortage and famine. At the conclusion of the tale he confesses his religious despair. The only other time he speaks, the king makes a violent vow to finish off the prophet for good.

Still, some have been able to generate sympathetic interpretations on the king's behalf. Indeed, these are really difficult circumstances for a ruler. He is not remiss in his concern. Twice we see him walking on top of the wall around the city. Perhaps he is personally surveying how bleak the situation really is as well as trying to come up with some options. After all, this is not an absentee monarch in a time of crisis. Even these two cannibal mothers, least likely of his citizens, appear to have direct access to him. Hence there are some grounds on which to defend the monarch, despite his hasty actions against Elisha. Given the impossible circumstances his vow to kill the prophet was likely a gesture of desperation. Indeed, he shows signs of real concern in his role as viceregent of the people before God.[2] After all, he wears sackcloth as a sign of lament and national repentance.[3] The overwhelming nature of the siege, the famine, and the unfathomable incident of cannibalism together mandate that the king do something. His expression of outrage in the form of an angry vow to kill Elisha, though hasty, was at least a response. And let's not forget, at the end of the story he does eventually come to his senses and revise his plan. In the end, when he confesses his lack of faith, it is not in the prophet but in God.[4]

But interpretations of the character of this king are not all so magnanimous. Some assessments are less forgiving and less gracious. He doesn't address the siege, the famine, or the women's crisis. On this score, when compared with other monarchs in the biblical tradition this king is found wanting. When compared with such figures as Solomon this king appears pathetic. When Solomon was confronted with the two harlot mothers fighting over the life of a child he issued an order and resolved their controversy (1 Kings 3:16-28). By contrast, this king does nothing to address the mothers' crisis. In response to the woman's request he issues no order. In contrast to Solomon's action, which results in the community's recognition of his wisdom, this king's inaction toward the two cannibal mothers invites

---

[2] Richard Nelson, *First and Second Kings.* Interpretation (Atlanta: John Knox, 1987) 189.

[3] Donald Wiseman, *1 and 2 Kings* (Leicester: InterVarsity, 1993) 211; John Gray, *I & II Kings. A Commentary* (Philadelphia: Westminster, 1963; 2nd rev. ed. 1970) 523.

[4] Gwilym Jones, *1 and 2 Kings.* 2 vols. New Century Bible Commentary (Grand Rapids: Eerdmans, 1984) 435.

the conclusion that he sorely lacks such a quality. Tearing his robes and vowing to slay the prophet are the only gestures he makes. His ability and power to address the real difficulties at hand—namely the siege, the famine, the women, to say nothing about the plight of the remaining child—are apparently nonexistent.[5] In the end he confesses his lack of faith in God, a faithlessness that contrasts with the faithfulness of Elisha.[6]

Across interpretations the controversy between these two characters, the king and the prophet, remains at center stage, consistently taking precedence over and eclipsing the urgent crisis and desperate controversy between the two women in this tale. When the women's crisis does receive attention it is but a means to other ends. First, it provides a motive for the king's hostility to Elisha. If we follow the story's progression, the vow to kill the prophet comes immediately on the heels of the woman's plea for help and the disclosure of the agreement she made with the other mother to eat their children. Hence, though never explicitly saying so, the story implies that the king's hostility toward the prophet is prompted by the crisis of the women. Next, the women's story has also been enlisted to illustrate the destructive behavior that prophets associate with rampant social breakdown.[7] The social conditions have become so grave that mothers are resorting even to eating their own children. Here the women become the signifier of how disconnected humans have become in relation to their own worth and value. Social decay has progressed to such a degree that mothers are alienated even from their maternal instinct.

Often the women's story has been interpreted as serving the larger purpose of the Deuteronomist. In the book of Deuteronomy eating the flesh of one's sons and daughters serves as a sign of infidelity.

> In the desperate straits to which the enemy siege reduces you, you will eat the fruit of your womb, the flesh of your own sons and daughters whom YHWH your God has given you. Even the most refined and gentle of men among you will begrudge food to his own brother, to the wife whom he embraces, and to the last of his remaining children, giving to none of them any of the flesh of his children whom he is eating, because nothing else remains to him, in the desperate straits to which the enemy siege will reduce you in all your towns. She who is

---

[5] Robert LaBarbera, "The Man of War and the Man of God: Social Satire in 2 Kings 6:8–7:20," *CBQ* 46 (1984) 646.

[6] Joseph Robinson, *The Second Book of Kings* (London, New York, and Melbourne: Cambridge University Press, 1976) 65.

[7] Stuart Lasine, "Jehoram and the Cannibal Mothers (2 Kings 6:24-33): Solomon's Judgment in an Inverted World," *JSOT* 50 (1991) 32–33.

the most refined and gentle among you, so gentle and refined that she does not venture to set the sole of her foot on the ground, will begrudge food to the husband whom she embraces, to her own son, and to her own daughter, begrudging even the afterbirth that comes out from between her thighs, and the children that she bears, because she is eating them in secret for lack of anything else, in the desperate straits to which the enemy siege will reduce you in your towns. (Deut 28:53-57)

Hence the mothers' story not only narrates and illustrates the desperation of Samaria's citizens;[8] the report of cannibalism serves as fulfillment of a Deuteronomic curse on disobedience. Here it garners a function beyond the confines of its brief story world. It functions to confirm the Deuteronomist's larger theological purpose.[9] Fidelity to covenant brings the rewards of prosperity and long life. Infidelity merits punishment in the form of death and destruction. Cannibalism graphically represents the extreme state of this destruction and decay. Hence the story of the cannibal mothers not only functions to provide the motive for hostility between king and prophet and as a sign of rampant social breakdown; it also works to illustrate the Deuteronomist theology of reward and punishment.

Some thirty years ago groups marginalized because of their race, gender, or social standing began teaching us to be wary of texts and interpretations that subjugate some characters or use them to promote a supposedly grand political or even theological vision such as that of the Deuteronomist. In our story the women clearly serve such a function. The groundbreaking work of such groups in biblical studies has not only drawn attention to the victimization of characters. By their work the nameless, faceless, minor characters have been emancipated from their shadowy moorings as "background." In the process dominant ways of reading have been challenged. "Background" figures have been revealed as characters deserving attention and interpretation. Due to the efforts of feminists' groups the recovery of women in the biblical writings has been a particularly persistent pursuit. As a result women have been liberated from their patriarchal anchor in the biblical writings and revealed as leaders, theologians, and religious models.

At the same time attention to these lesser characters has made some unsettling disclosures. The Bible convulses with victims, many of them women, who have been subjugated by the very story in which they are featured. The unnamed lieutenant in the account immediately following our

---

[8] LaBarbera, "The Man of War and the Man of God," 647.
[9] Ibid. 646.

tale is illustrative. In predicting the end of the siege and famine Elisha foretells that this guard at the gate of the city will not live to witness the return of domestic tranquility to Samaria (7:2). When the people return from the abandoned Syrian camp loaded with foodstuffs they trample this soldier to death in their haste and impatience (7:20). Here this unnamed civil servant and his death function to demonstrate the credibility of the prophetic word. But they demonstrate more. They indicate who is expendable and who is not.

This keeper of the gate at Samaria is not alone. He stands alongside many other characters in the biblical tradition who appear expendable. Tamar, the daughter of David, was raped by her half-brother Amnon (2 Sam 13:1-22), but the future and fate of Tamar are lost in the stories that follow. Instead the traditions focus on the enmity between brothers resulting from this deed. In the book of Judges, Jephthah sacrifices his daughter as the result of a faithless vow he made in order to secure from God a victory in battle (Judg 11:29-40). Who this virgin daughter was we will never know. Lot, in his effort to protect male visitors to his house, is ready to offer his virgin daughters to the men of the village beating on his door and demanding access to these newcomers (Gen 19:1-11). If the roster of unnamed or expendable victims in the biblical traditions could be tallied, the legacy of violence would loom large. Regrettably, the unnamed mothers in our story must be added to this list. At first glance one might object that mothers who boil and eat their children qualify as the doers of violence rather than its victims. Indeed, at face value cannibalism is a repugnant and desperate act. The cannibalizing of their own children makes these women's deed even more difficult to deal with. Moreover, in the face of the impending threat to the second child it seems especially reprehensible that the woman may be asking the monarch to require the other mother to keep her word. But attention to the issues of power embedded in this tale suggests otherwise and reveals that not only children but also the women are the real victims being consumed here.

Like new literary criticism, a postmodern assessment notes that three crises structure the story in 2 Kings 6:24-33: the crisis between Israel and Syria, the conflict between the king and the prophet, and the problem between the two mothers. However, in this current appraisal we attend to an unevenness in the narrative in the treatment of the three crises. While the conflict between Israel and Syria and that between the king and the prophet are addressed, the difficulty between the two mothers is not. Attention to this anomaly exposes other irregularities in our tale.

We have seen that in conventional literary assessments characters who have the most to say often weigh in as major characters. However, another anomaly in this tale requires that we ignore such conventions. Though the cannibal mother has more words to recite than anyone else in this short story, both her social position and the dynamics of power in patriarchal writings make her voice all but inaudible. Instead, as introduction to her story the narrator spotlights the privileged parties, Ben-Hadad and the king in Israel. Ben-Hadad has marched his army and laid siege to the city (6:24). The king of Israel, challenged by the threat, is walking on the wall, surveying the besieged city (6:26a). The story of the mothers (6:26b-29) intervenes and discloses the crisis this international power struggle has wrought. But the woman's request is bothersome and interrupts the king's stroll. When the king responds we are reminded that he is still on the wall above her (6:30). The hierarchic class relations in the social order are made clear in the spatial description. His recitation of a vow (6:31) turns attention away from the crisis of the starving women and toward a different power struggle—the contest between king and prophet. The story concludes with a focus on the prophet surrounded by the elders (6:32-33). Hence the three crises and their inherent struggles across this story structure the tale as follows:

v. 24 Ben-Hadad and his army

Authorities in a struggle
for international power

v. 26 Israel's king walking on the
wall of the city

vv. 27-29 Woman and her story            Mothers in a struggle for a
child's life as food

v. 30 Israel's king walking on the
wall of the city

Authorities in a struggle
vv. 31-33 Prophet and elders            for national power

The woman's story is the centerpiece of this chiastic arrangement. Still, she is not at center stage. At best she is but the marginalized protagonist. Her struggle for food and the child's life is dwarfed and rendered insignificant by the magnitude of the national and international struggles for power that surround her. Irony works within this power field of kings and prophets, exposing it in order to contest it. Sandwiched between these contestants vying for domination and control, the mothers and their unresolved crisis are being swallowed up by the privileged struggles surrounding them. Despite what the mother reports about the women's cannibalizing activities, the mothers and their children are being consumed by the insatiable cravings of these political and religious leaders.

While the mother has the most to say, what she says does not count. Hegemonic discourse, or the interchanges of those with power, competes with and overrides the maternal speech here. While the woman's story sets forth a crisis that is immediate and urgent, her narrative warrants no resolution. Its outcome remains unknown. As the story unfolds, the conflict between those in power, the king and the prophet, remains at the forefront and quickly overrides the women's dilemma. Such a dynamic is not confined to the biblical narrative. Representations that privilege the powerful abound in our own time as well.

Some years ago an issue of the *San Francisco Chronicle* carried a report on the continued controversy between the Tutsi and Hutu of Rwanda.[10] A graphic photo of a dying four-year-old Tutsi child with his grieving mother slumped over him in the remains of a deserted refugee camp in Burundi accompanied the headline "Burundi Steps Up Expulsions of Rwandans." The article reviewed the history of the controversy and offered an update of the battle between leaders and the warring factions of the two ethnic groups. The response of other nations and the United Nations' gestures were also sketched. Nowhere in the report was a reference to the mother and child or what happened to them. In fact, the impact of the report served to distract and to nullify any feeling that might be evoked in response to the photo. The matter-of-fact nature of the report and the spotlighting of the larger controversy between important leaders and their crisis seemed to anesthetize the reader to the incredible personal suffering and sadness of the refugees as well as to obscure the victim mother and child. The following day's report continued to map the crisis between warring factions. As we have learned to expect, no mention was made of the child or his mother. They were but a graphic prop, a sensational summons for the truly newsworthy controversy, the conflict between those in power.

Such a photo is not unique. Daily we witness scores of nameless faces of victims on our TV screens, on the Internet, or in our newspapers. Refugees, starving children, uprooted villagers in wartime all signal our attention and court our response. However, more often than not the accompanying story makes no mention of these individuals. Rather, we hear about the struggles of those in power over them, those in charge of their livelihood, and those who control the economics that determine their well-being. The narrative of the cannibal mothers' plight functions in a similar fashion. With other stories, it forms the thematic backdrop of a larger tale. In the complex of the larger narrative (6:24–7:20) the episode of the canni-

---

[10] Corrine Dufka, "Burundi Steps Up Expulsions of Rwandans," *San Francisco Chronicle* (23 July 1996) A8.

bal mothers is subsumed into a category of references that portray the prevailing ecological conditions of starvation. The high prices in the markets, Elisha's prediction of the decrease in food prices by the morrow, the urgent hunger expressed by the lepers, and the stampede for food at the end join with the episode of the cannibal mothers to serve as background against which the main plot of the story is painted. The mothers' controversy, their starvation, their desperation, and the threat to the second child's life are never addressed, never resolved, or never returned to in the grander literary scheme. Instead, the mothers serve the interests of another form of controversy, a privileged controversy, that constitutes the heart of the story. The struggle between the waywardness of the king and the prowess of the prophet occupies center stage; it is acted out in bold relief against the backdrop of the suffering citizens whose plight is but a secondary crisis that is obscured and eventually lost in the telling.

What such literary seams and anomalies disclose, anthropological studies confirm. Cannibalism is tied to the experience of famine in this story, but famine does not explain the cannibalism. Cannibalism is never just about eating. It is not just a response to extreme hunger, as materialistic theories have proposed.[11] Many tribal and post-tribal societies that hunger do not resort to cannibalism. Ecological and demographic factors that lead to famine and hence to cannibalism in some societies do not provoke this practice in others.

Cannibalism is a cultural practice, and it varies in meaning with each cultural context.[12] As such it is culturally constituted and laden with nongustatory messages. While hunger is recognized as its motivation, it is secondary to larger concerns. Recent anthropological studies identify the overarching ethos of a cultural system as often standing in direct relationship to a community's response in times of food stress.[13] In societies where accommodation and integration with cosmic and social forces preside, cannibalism is nonexistent. Harmony and integration perdure, particularly in the constructs of politics, government, and social order. Myths, rituals,

---

[11] For example see Michael Harner, "The Ecological Basis for Aztec Sacrifice," *American Ethnologist* 4 (1979) 117–35; Michael Harris, *Cannibals and Kings: The Origins of Cultures* (New York: Random House, 1977), who propose hunger and protein deficiency as explanations for human sacrifice among the Aztec.

[12] For a study of the practice and significance of cannibalism as related to particular cultures see the collection of essays in Pamela Brown and Don Tuzin, *The Ethnography of Cannibalism* (Washington, D.C.: The Society for Psychological Anthropology, 1983).

[13] For an extended study of cannibalism as tied to the prevailing ethos of a cultural system see Peggy Reeves Sanday, *Divine Hunger—Cannibalism as a Cultural System* (Cambridge and New York: Cambridge University Press, 1986).

and symbols tend to reflect these constructs and thus predicate and reinforce an abiding sociopolitical framework of tranquility and equality.[14]

By contrast, control and domination reign as the presiding mores in societies where cannibalism is practiced. The types of leadership, political structure, and social configuration express these prevailing constructs. Often these communities can claim a once-harmonious social order that has subsequently broken down. Reciprocal relations between persons and with nature have been replaced by hierarchical forms of governance. In these circumstances cannibalism may be part of a hegemonic strategy developed in reaction to a perceived threat from natural or political forces. In other instances it may be a response by those subject to or oppressed by controlling hierarchical forces in threatening circumstances.[15] Hence the presence of cannibalism or its absence appears not to be the direct consequence of scarcity of food but specifically associated with the prevailing ethos of a society. Where accommodation and harmony are subordinate to or replaced by domination and control, cannibalism may constitute a response to famine.[16]

Cannibalism as tied to hunger, therefore, is far more complex than simple cause and effect. Rather, its existence is yoked to a prevailing sociopolitical structure of domination and control. The hunger for food that would motivate citizens to cannibalize coincides with sovereigns' voracious appetites for power and domination. The insatiable craving on the

---

[14] For example, the Mbuti of the Ituri Forest in the Northeast Congo are guided by a worldview that is antithetical to the governing strategies and social configuration of domination, mastery, and control over nature. Each individual is imbued with a life force, derivative of a larger source embodied by the forest on which their life depends. Harmony with forces of nature as embodied in nature and by each individual is essential to the well-being of the society. Physical violence as a response to famine or as a means to resolving a dispute would be tantamount to sacrilege. Moreover, when faced with the prospects of enduring famine the Mbuti believe that order and harmony have been disrupted and require reinstatement. For example, when hunting and fishing fail the Mbuti conduct a ceremony that addresses potential oppositions within the community—oppositions between male and female, chaos and order, forest and camp. This ethos of harmony and integration in the wake of an absence of food among other comparable societies such as the Navajo, the people of Tidopia and Ik also coincide with an absence of cannibalism. See Sanday, *Divine Hunger* 214–31.

[15] The social and political order of both the Aztec and Iroquois (especially the Huron) was constituted in terms of struggle and control. Cannibalism and sacrifice were primordial metaphors that symbolized domination and submission, the ethos of these societies. The magnitude of the sacrifice and torture complex associated with cannibalism increased sharply in response to drought, famine, and competition among Indian groups in the face of European expansion. See Sanday, *Divine Hunger* 125–50, and Marshall Sahlins, "Culture as Protein and Profit," *New York Review of Books* 25 (1978) 45–53.

[16] Sanday, *Divine Hunger* 54–55.

part of the powerful reigns over the hunger of the powerless, who eventually resort to cannibalizing in the face of threat. Tragically, the lives and destinies of the powerless, often women and children, are the carcasses left behind as debris from the escapades of the powerful. As with the women and children of Afghanistan, Palestine, the Two-Thirds World, or even the poor working class in this country, the well-being and futures of expendable persons are consumed and obliterated by the promotion of the livelihood and destiny of an already privileged class. However, the fate of the powerless goes virtually unnoticed. The social framework that supports hegemonies of power and privilege effectively relegates these masses, in this case these women, to the status of "other."

The act of imaging identity is, at the same time, the act of authoring difference in the act of constructing this "other." It is an act of distinguishing and separating from others. The process is complex. On the one hand the act of defining oneself is negative. One is by virtue of who one is not. On the other hand those outsiders who are needed for one's very self-definition are at the same time regarded as the threat. Ironically, once the outsiders are established they are defined as the threat to the boundaries that are composed to exclude them. Yet it is only the conceptualization of their status as "outsider" that maintains these boundaries. Outside, by definition, is always threatening to get in. These "others" are poised in a delicate balance that is always off balance because fear and aggression continually weight the scales.

In the case of these biblical women their only identity, "cannibal mothers," makes them particularly objectionable and ensures their "otherness."[17] Portraying the women as eaters of their own children effectively obscures their status as victims and immunizes almost everyone against the sympathies their plight evokes. Moreover, their brief and delimited identification as "cannibalizing mothers" elicits shock, gasp, and rapt attention that curtail notice of the more gluttonous consumptions on the part of those responsible for the women's horrific circumstances.

Whether the story of the two cannibal mothers was constructed as pro-monarchic narrative in support of the institution of kingship or composed to serve the Deuteronomistic purpose of indicting the monarchy, it takes for granted the complex of hegemonic rule. Even if we resist identifying the historical setting of this tale, the story world presumes a monarchic setting.

[17] Reading colonial and postcolonial literature has helped shape my understanding of the parallels between women and other colonized subjects, both of whom are easily relegated to the position of "other," colonized by various kinds of patriarchal domination. See especially the collection of essays in Bill Ashcroft, Gareth Griffiths, and Helen Tiffin, eds., *The Post-Colonial Studies Reader* (London and New York: Routledge, 1995).

Elements within the tale and within the larger surrounding narrative sketch a monarchic milieu and its accompanying patriarchal ideology of domination and control.

Power and privilege reside in the hands of dominant males. The king, the sovereign in Israel, rules the nation and vies with the prophet for domains beyond his control. Elisha, the religious official of YHWH who controls the elements of nature, poses one among several threats to the monarch's power. Consistent with this ethos, the inevitable stresses that power and privilege create are visited upon the less powerful. The citizens of Samaria are starving as a result of controversy between powerful kings and the subsequent conflict between Israel's king and its powerful prophet. Conditions are so serious that these two mothers have resorted to eating their own children. But the maintenance of a culture of power and domination requires that those responsible for systemic injustice be shielded from responsibility.[18] Hence, when confronted with the gravity of his subjects' situation, the king blames both God and the prophet. He distances himself from the victims and from the violence that has resulted from the present military conditions by expressing moral indignation. He tears his garment and exposes his sackcloth while pronouncing a vow to kill the prophet. Such expressions of moral indignation obscure and distract attention from the responsibility of those in power. At the same time these gestures are a cover for such rulers' inability to address the immediacy of the crisis. Moreover, expressions of moral outrage serve to obscure violence or even to justify more violence on the part of those with power to address the infraction.

Gil Bailie's recap of the United States government's policies during wartime reflects this kinship between expressions of moral indignation and subsequent acts of violence.

> When the Japanese bombed Shanghai in 1937, moral revulsion in the U.S. was strong. When the fascists bombed Barcelona in 1938, Cordell Hull, the U.S. Secretary of State, declared: "No theory of war can justify such conduct." In June of 1938, the U.S. Senate passed a resolution condemning the "inhuman bombing of civilian populations." Following the outbreak of war, one of Franklin Roosevelt's first pronouncements was an appeal to the belligerents to refrain from bombing civilian populations. By 1944, however, the bombing of German

---

[18] I am especially grateful to Mary Ann Tolbert for her essay "Reading for Liberation," in Fernando Segovia and Mary Ann Tolbert, eds., *Reading From This Place* (Minneapolis: Fortress, 1995) 1:263–76, in which she explores the consequences of patriarchal hegemony for its subjects and for readers/interpreters of the Bible.

cities had the backing of military strategists, and in August of 1945 atomic bombs were dropped on Hiroshima and Nagasaki.[19]

Hence expressions of moral indignation apparently serve to foreshadow or coincide with the duplication of the violence rather than the curtailing of it. Coupled with this rapidly progressing pathology is the blindness on the part of those most outraged. They fail to see the reflection of the violence they condemn in the violence they enlist to address the situation. In our story the king addresses the transgression of cannibalizing children with a public promise to headhunt the prophet. The structural similarity between the violence he loathes and the violence he vows is revealing.

In hegemonic society the violence that maintains and characterizes the ruling structure cultivates and necessitates violence among its citizens. Recipients of the violence, the powerless, trade violence among themselves as the only currency with which to purchase survival. The poor live in run-down neighborhoods that become the target for further violence. On this score they are also an easy target for judgment and blame on the part of the rich who live elsewhere. Further, the violence between citizens often warrants a judgment from the ruling powers that in turn sentences its citizens with further violence. Bailey's description of violence as "a-mazing" is apt. As the all-pervasive consequence of hegemonic rule, "the paths that seem to exit from [violence's] madness so often lead deeper into its maze."[20]

Violence unchecked does not confine itself to the political or judicial arena but seeks companionship and endorsement in religious spheres. It is no surprise, then, that the king's violent vow that accompanies his expression of moral indignation is carried out with religious overtones. When the king tears his robes he visibly displays sackcloth beneath his royal garments. The practice of wearing sackcloth, often adopted by biblical kings in times of threatened disaster, is commonly accompanied by fasting.[21] Not only does this disclosure on the part of the king derail any potential inquiry as to his responsibility for the women's problem; it probably also invites praise for his religious fervor and recognition of his concern for his citizens. But out of the seams of the story erupts an ironic contrast that protests. We now know not only what the king wears but also what he has on beneath his royal garments. By contrast, we have no direct information about the women's attire or appearance. Despite this narrative oversight, the king's initial response to the woman's cry, blaming God for the famine,

---

[19] Gil Bailie, *Violence Unveiled* (New York: Crossroad, 1995) 90.

[20] Ibid. 90.

[21] See for example, 1 Kings 21:27 or Jonah 3:5, 8-9.

suggests how they look: starving. Moreover, the woman's account of eating her own child confirms and further sketches her undescribed appearance: groveling, emaciated, desperate. The economic violence that constitutes the heart of hegemonic culture now reveals itself in the hypocrisy of religious practice. While Samaria's citizens are starving from a lack of food, the king is fasting from food.

Thus far we have been concerned with the implied abuse of power and the violence it unleashes on the powerless of a society. Would that the ethos of violence afflicting and subjugating these two mothers was confined to the social world of this story or even to the poetics that construct this tale! Unfortunately, such violence resonates and rebounds across generations in the form of responses to the text and in the prevailing ethos supporting such readings. Here the violence perpetrated against these women finds an accomplice in the history of interpretation.

Commentaries and studies of 2 Kings 6:24-33 vary little in their overall assessment of these cannibal mothers. First, it is significant to note that many interpretations cooperate with the story line and ignore the women altogether. When studies do address the women's presence and role in the tale they tend to do so along two lines. Many studies confine their assessment to contextualizing the cannibalistic practices. In these investigations cannibalism is explained as well-attested in times of siege.[22] Cannibalism is a condition prompted by a lack of food resulting from the threatening military circumstances. More often than not food stress created by a military assault is viewed as punishment from God. In addition, such studies tend to diffuse the horror of the reference to cannibalism in our story by citing other Old Testament instances that reference parents eating their children in exceptionally grave circumstances.[23] For example, in Ezek 5:10 the prophet speaks to the exiles in Babylon who were among the first to be deported, addressing their refusal to believe that punishment for infidelity is on the way. He lists the conditions that will befall the people left in the land of Judah; among them is cannibalism within families. "Surely, parents shall eat their children in your midst, and children shall eat their parents" (5:10). Later, in Lam 2:20 and 4:10 such images recur. Here images of mothers eating their children alongside a litany of other horrific conditions acknowledge the guilt and deepseated remorse of the people in exile.

---

[22] See Jonas Greenfield, *Storia e Tradizioni di Israele* (Bressia: Paideia Editrice, 1991) 125; Gray, *I & II Kings* 523; Jones, *1 and 2 Kings* 433; James Montgomery, *A Critical and Exegetical Commentary on the Books of Kings*, ed. Henry Gehman. International Critical Commentary (Edinburgh: T & T Clark, 1951) 385; Wiseman, *1 and 2 Kings* 211; Mordechai Cogan and Hayim Tadmor, *II Kings*. AB 11 (New York: Doubleday, 1988) 80.

[23] Deut 28:56-57; Ezek 5:10; Lam 2:20; 4:10.

Charged with pathos, these confessions are enveloped in expressions of repentance and remorse.

In addition, studies that contextualize the reference to cannibalism often do so by reference to other ancient societies. Ample examples from comparative literature further reinforce the widespread and commonplace nature of cannibalism beyond Israel in the ancient Near East.[24] Such comparisons, while not discounting the unacceptable nature of such a practice, serve to reduce the horror of its citation. Hence such studies situate cannibalism in such a way as to explain its presence in Israel as related to its occurrence in the larger ancient Near Eastern world.

The other focus across interpretations fixes on the women themselves and frames the women's portrait with a barrage of condemnation. First, the women are condemned for their participation in cannibalism. On this score descriptions such as "abominable," "callous," "shameless," "inhuman" constitute the women's notoriety. Next, the woman complainant before the king is singled out. She is accused of lacking not only public shame but also compassion. Here the woman is not given the benefit of the doubt. Interpretation assumes that she is asking the king to use his judicial authority to force the other woman to keep her word. But if we pay close attention to her speech we see that she does not specify why she beseeches the king. She cries out to him for help, explaining that they are so hungry that they have cannibalized one of the children and in the process a controversy has erupted between them. She may have been seeking his assistance to force the other woman to make good on her word. However, she may also have been telling the king the story in order to confront the highest authority with how very serious circumstances had become for citizens. Her plea to him for help seems more likely a very desperate cry to do something about the dire conditions of starvation. The horror of her circumstances and deeds certainly catches our attention. Perhaps confronting the king with the story of something so grave as mothers eating their own children would finally incite this king to do something. After all, this degree of famine did not materialize overnight. The narrative would have us believe that the enemy siege must have been very long and successful for hunger to become so grave. Moreover, the narrative gives no indication whether the

---

[24] Josephus' record of the practice at the time of the Roman siege of Jerusalem (*Jewish War* vi. 3.4), and the instances of cannibalism during Ashurbanipal's siege of Babylon (Daniel David Luckenbill, *Ancient Records of Assyria and Babylonia* [New York: Greenwood Press, 1968] 2:190; A. L. Oppenheim, "Siege Documents from Nippur," *Iraq* 17 [1955] 69–70) are often cited. See Jones, *1 and 2 Kings* 433; Wiseman, *1 and 2 Kings* 211; Cogan and Tadmor, *II Kings* 80; Montgomery, *A Critical and Exegetical Commentary* 385; Gray, *I & II Kings* 523.

king has done anything thus far to counter the siege or whether he has done anything to address the incredible circumstances of his citizens. Hence this woman's story is not only a testimony of how desperate life had become; it may also indicate how ineffective or even inactive the king has been. In either case it is the woman and her story that finally prompt him to do something. And while the king's vow to behead the prophet hardly bespeaks political savvy or a military scheme, it does move the crisis beyond the stultifying impasse and eventually to a resolution. This mother's audacious confrontation of the king with her own lamentable straits finally stirs the king to act. However, no one in the story or in the history of interpretation has ever acknowledged the role played by this mother and her admission before the king. She is condemned for her deeds and discounted as having no significant part to play in this tale.

The other mother, who is only briefly mentioned in the narrative, also receives condemnation. She too is indicted for cannibalism. In addition, some studies fault her further for not keeping her word. Hence when the character of the women is commented upon, the condemnation of them is comprehensive. While one woman is accused of deception, the other is indicted for showing no compunction for what she has done.[25]

The outcome of each part of this analysis—the practice of cannibalism and the mothers as practicing cannibalism—when placed alongside one another is revelatory. However, it reveals far more about the commitments of the history of interpretation than it does about the story. While the practice of cannibalism in the ancient world of the Bible is depicted as understandable, the women's behavior is not. While the respectability of the biblical narrative is preserved for what it reports, the women's respectability is not. In subtle but nevertheless successful ways the tradition of interpretation preserves the integrity of the Bible in reporting an incident of cannibalism by sacrificing what is left of the women's humanity because they practice cannibalism. Hence the violence done to the women in the text does not confine itself to the story world. The history of interpretation participates in preserving not only the text but the violence and its victims therein.

Recent interpretations tend to wrestle more self-consciously and respectfully with the place of the cannibal mothers in this tale. Here the crisis of the mothers is not understood to indict them. Rather their story is judged as the exponent of just how morally depraved biblical Israel has become. "Indeed, a mother whose maternal instinct has failed symbolizes a world in

---

[25] Lasine, "Jehoram and the Cannibal Mothers" 28, 38–39; Hugh Pyper, "Judging the Wisdom of Solomon: The Two-Way Effect of Intertextuality," *JSOT* 59 (1993) 26.

chaos."[26] Hence the women's story becomes the ledger upon which the moral status of the community is assessed. Yet such insights in the wrong hands can still deliver a fateful blow to these women. The labyrinth of violence turns back in serpentine fashion and victimizes by villainizing them. Is it the women's desperate but despicable deed or their current state of degradation that serves as exponent for the society's moral decay? Do they represent moral disintegration as its accomplice or as its victim?

The larger narrative world of the tale presumes a patriarchal society. Surrounding the women, kings battle with other kings leaving a trail of bloodshed. In the time of Elisha the Jehu dynasty overthrows the Omri dynasty. The prophet supports these events by instructing the aspiring candidate to the throne to slay the entire reigning family. At the same time male monarchs headhunt male prophets. Ahab orders all the prophets of YHWH to be killed. Elijah, YHWH's prophet, in turn slaughters four hundred fifty Baal prophets in the Wadi Kishon. Moreover, this enmity between leagues of prophets is tied to and encouraged by the enmity between those struggling to seize power as kings. Allied with the antagonisms between prophets and between candidates to the throne are the struggles between male deities who contest one another's phallic potency and prowess in nature. The battles between YHWH and Baal are intimately related to the struggles among humans for domination and control. Hence the battles of politics and religion are intimately ensnared with the rhetoric of theological warfare.

As exponent of social decay does this lone story of controversy between two starving women over the life of a child adequately represent the prevailing life-threatening antics of prophets and kings? Does it really function to disclose how utterly sinful this society has become? Or does it reveal something else? Does it indicate instead who the victims are? Unnamed, the women are without identity. That they cannot be tied to any family robs them not only of identity but of all hope. That they confront the king while he walks on the wall situates them in the outer limits of the city. Here we are given a hint of who they might be. Living among those who inhabit the walls of the city, they are geographically the marginalized. Socially they are the outcast. Resorting to the extreme of cannibalizing their own children, the women disclose their utter desperation in the face of starvation. Surrendering their maternal instinct, they become alienated from one of the only roles for women that patriarchal society recognizes. Agreeing to eat their own offspring, the women must abandon their own destiny.

---

[26] Claudia Camp, "1 and 2 Kings," in Carol A. Newsom and Sharon H. Ringe, eds., *The Women's Bible Commentary* (London: S.P.C.K.; Louisville: Westminster John Knox, 1992) 108.

No, the women do not so much represent social and moral decay as they stand as the victims of these parasitic conditions. Consuming their own flesh and blood, the women sacrifice their own destiny. Thus they and their children represent an expiatory offering bearing the iniquities of the whole society. Here humanity appears so compromised that it must seek the maintenance of its life in the death of its own flesh and blood. That the mothers agree to consume their own flesh and blood is not so much an indictment of them as villains; rather it is evidence of their own annihilation as victims.

While the narrator of this story and the history of interpretation have worked to trivialize these women and their plight, our study of their character indicates that this is no trivial matter. These mothers and their tale have taught us many disturbing lessons about power and violence—lessons that we could not have accessed if we fixed solely upon the king and the prophet. Our study of the mothers' character has also taught us something about interpretation and about life itself. They have made us confront what is lost when only the so-called "major" characters are studied or when only the people deemed important by cultural standards are considered. As the fullness of meaning in a biblical tale increases when each and every character is assessed, so too is the fullness of life itself extended when each person is regarded as worthy of attention. But the harvest of our study of these two unnamed women does not stop here. Our study of them reveals a kind of exploitation of character that echoes across the biblical tradition. As our study of their story illuminates other biblical tales we will see this dangerous dynamic at work in other biblical characters.

# CHAPTER FIVE

## *Stories Speak of Other Stories*

Unlike the detail and description accompanying major characters, we have very little information about our two cannibal mothers. Contrary to conventional methods for character building, the narrative offers no description of how the women looked or dressed. It gives no hint of the women's inner lives or even information regarding their identities. Still, in the preceding chapter we saw how attending to seams and disjunctions in the texts might grant us some sense of their identity and their plight. We also considered how the dominant role of the king and prophet distracted attention from the women's story and how the conflict between those with power victimizes these women as well as others like them. Further, our review of studies on cannibalism revealed that this response in times of food shortage coincides with those oppressive conditions cultivated by hierarchical configurations of society and the ethos of patriarchy. As result, the outcome of our research levels its judgment not against the women but against the king and the prophet—and issues a warning as well. The long history of interpretation that shortsightedly indicts these mothers deserves its own indictment. But we can say more. This story of powerless mothers can disclose its power by illuminating the circumstances and encumbrances of other similar characters. In the process other tales may further our understanding of these two mothers and even build character in us.

It is true that the scarcity of references challenges what depth of understanding can be achieved here. But while the silence surrounding such characters fails to yield direct information, the context does provide clues. In the opening chapters we noted how this story in 2 Kings 6:24-33 does not reside alone but is enmeshed in a larger mosaic of stories. However, this network is not limited to the Elisha tradition or even the Deuteronomistic history. Rather our story, like all stories in the Bible, is part of a larger framework. Together with many other tales it constitutes and composes what eventually becomes the "canon" of Sacred Scripture. "Canon," literally meaning "measuring line" or "rule," refers to the final fixed form and collection of books. While the actual decision process and date for the establishment of the Old Testament canon is highly debated, many suggest a time around 90 C.E. The collection was established on the consensus that together these books express the faith beliefs of communities claiming them as their confessional texts. "Together" here is the operative word. The notion of canon is important for us because it suggests a further context for our story. It urges us to read and understand our tale *together* with other stories of the canon. Inevitably, as we do the reading, other stories, even our own stories, come into play. Hence our character building exercise now shows its potential to extend itself and raise challenges for us in our world.

In a tale where little is told about characters the links and enmeshments with this larger collation of stories become very significant. As the context is broadened to include the whole canon, parallels and contrasts with other stories can shed light on these two mothers and their crisis. At the same time this brief account of the two mothers struggling over the life of a child joins with similar stories disclosing insights and understanding about other persons in such straits.

In this chapter we will study some tales that shed light on this character-building exercise. We will take up three stories that bear a resemblance to our cannibal mothers episode. In each of these instances two women in crisis struggle over the matter of a child. In the first story two women appear before a king and debate who is the true mother of a living child. In the second instance Sarah and her maidservant Hagar are set in opposition over the matter of the conception of a child. In the third case two sisters, Rachel and Leah, are also at odds over the matter of the birth of a child.

None of the stories claim to be exact parallels. Indeed, each of the stories is distinct. The crises between the women arise for various reasons. The relations between the women in each instance are different. Still, each pair displays parallels and contrasts with our cannibal mothers' story, and with one another, that assist our character building exercise both for these mothers and for ourselves. In addition, our horizons about biblical characters and what we can know about them are broadened. Across these exchanges we not only learn about the cannibal mothers but about these other characters and their stories as well. And as these stories speak of other stories and these characters speak about other characters, they might even speak about us.

## Two Women before Solomon (1 Kings 3:16-28)

In this first story two women bring their dispute over the life of a child before a king. In the account immediately preceding, King Solomon has just awakened from a dream in which he was granted wisdom. Though the king is not named in the account we are considering, most traditions interpret the monarch to be Solomon.

As the story opens the two women are identified as "prostitutes." Prostitution was a commonly recognized institution in Israel and in the ancient Near East,[1] as other biblical stories confirm. To be a prostitute or to behave as one is not necessarily an indictment on a woman's character. For example, Tamar was the wife of Judah's sons, both of whom died (Genesis 38). According to Israelite law a man from the dead husband's family must provide offspring for the widow. When Judah fails to provide a third son as husband for Tamar she disguises herself as a prostitute and becomes pregnant by her father-in-law in order to force on him responsibility for the legacy of his dead son (Genesis 38). In another story Israelite spies are scouting out Jericho in order to plan a strategy of attack (Joshua 2). Rahab, a prostitute who lives in the wall surrounding the city, provides refuge for the spies. In return for her hospitality Rahab and her family are spared destruction, and they are allowed to settle among the Israelites (Josh 6:25). In Lev 21:7, 14 the law prohibits a priest from marrying a harlot. Here the need to legislate on this matter serves as evidence of the fact that others in Israel do wed prostitutes. Hence the identification of the two women before the king in 1 Kings 3 as "prostitutes" is not a judgment but a characterization.[2] Like cannibalism, prostitution in context warrants no indictment.

When the first woman speaks she explains how the kinship between the two women has been severed by a tragedy in the night. They live together in a house and were both pregnant at the same time. They gave birth only three days apart. While they were sleeping, the other woman lay on her child and the infant died. Upon discovering the misfortune she exchanged her dead baby for the other woman's child. When the first woman awoke in the morning to nurse her son she found the child was dead. When she examined him more closely in the light of day she discovered that he was not the son whom she bore.

Next the other woman speaks. However, when she does so she merely argues to the contrary. "No, the living son is mine, and the dead son is yours" (3:22a). Immediately the first woman responds by reversing the allegation:

---

[1] Phyllis Bird, "The Harlot as Heroine: Narrative Art and Social Presupposition in Three Old Testament Texts," *Semeia* 46 (1989) 32.

[2] Phyllis Trible, *God and the Rhetoric of Sexuality* (Philadelphia: Fortress, 1978) 31.

"No, the dead son is yours, and the living son is mine" (3:22b). Hence their quarrel over the life of the child creates a forensic deadlock.

When the king finally speaks he simply rehearses their verbal impasse. "The one says, 'This is my son that is alive, and your son is dead'; while the other says, 'Not so! Your son is dead, and my son is the living one'" (3:23). When he finally speaks his own mind he orders that a sword be fetched and brought before him. Next he commands that the living child be divided in two so that half can be given to one woman and half can be given to the other.

The king is obviously counting on maternal instinct to kick in and end the impasse, which it does. The first woman wells up with compassion for her child and blurts out to surrender her son: "Please, my lord, give her the living boy; certainly do not kill him!" (3:26). The king responds by repeating her words and ending the impasse, "Give the first woman the living boy; do not kill him" (3:27). As the story concludes, the narrator avers that all Israel is in awe of this king and his judgment. The wisdom that Solomon had received in the preceding episode is now recognized as dwelling within him. Hence what starts out as a story of two women in crisis over a child becomes a story about a king and his wisdom. No mention is made of the mother's incredible gesture of self-sacrifice. No heed is given to the fact that the king's success depended on the response of the woman to her maternal instinct. No attention is paid to the matter that the king's words of assessment, "Give the first woman the living boy; do not kill him" (3:27), are a mere parroting of the mother's audacious exclamation. "Please, my lord, give her the living boy; certainly do not kill him" (3:26). Moreover, no thought is given to what might have happened if the king's strategy had failed.

The analogical connections between this tale and the story of our cannibal mothers are easily mapped. Both tales involve two nameless women, each of whom has given birth to a son. In both instances one of the children has died and a controversy has erupted over the well-being of the remaining child. In each tale the pairs of women set forth their crises before the ruling monarch. Though the character of the women and their plight constitute the parallels, it is on the character of the king that most studies of these parallels focus. A comparison of the kings' responses and their ability to judge governs the heart of most investigations. Hence, in complete cooperation with the narrator, studies fix upon the king and ignore the victims.

For example, Stuart Lasine considers the differences in the portraits of the kings. He argues that "with god-like wisdom, [Solomon] can use his knowledge of the maternal nature to reveal the truth in a difficult case by exposing the true character of the disputants."[3] Though he assesses Solomon

---

[3] Stuart Lasine, "Jehoram and the Cannibal Mothers (2 Kings 6:24-33): Solomon's Judgment in an Inverted World," *JSOT* 50 (1991) 27–53.

as resourceful, Lasine does not conclude that by contrast the king in 2 Kings 6:24-33 is inept. Rather, he argues that in the later story the cannibal mother speaking in 2 Kings 6 overturns all expectations of maternal nature and puts the king in an impossible situation. Hence he tears his robes, exposes the sackcloth he is wearing, and with good reason assents to despair. For Lasine, 2 Kings 6 problematizes the nature of mothers and of God. Indeed, mothers eating their children does pose a hazard for society at large. But what is worse, a God who fails to end the siege and the accompanying famine might even be the force behind such unthinkable deeds. For Lasine this "topsy-turvy" world devoid of maternal instinct and ruled by a God who cannot be counted on qualifies as comedy.[4] Hence Lasine exonerates the king in 2 Kings 6 for his lack of action on behalf of the women, explaining that not even Solomon could have rendered wise judgment in such straits. It is worth noting that while Lasine observes the surface similarities between the women and their tale as the basis of his reading these stories together, his study attends more closely to a comparison of the monarchs rather than the women.

In another investigation Hugh Pyper also considers the relationship between the 2 Kings 6 story and the 1 Kings 3 account and takes a different position than Lasine.[5] However, his disagreement is not with Lasine's focus of attention on the monarch but with the conclusion he comes to. Instead of perceiving a contrast between the two kings and their situations Pyper argues that 2 Kings 6

> may actually be Solomon's world with the skin off, so to speak, a world where the assumptions and pretensions of kings are shown up for what they are—a world where Solomon's unbending harshness, epitomized in his willingness to divide the child, has led to the division of his kingdom under his son Rehoboam, whose weak attempts at bully tactics are a parody in themselves of his father's strength.[6]

It is true. Solomon had ambitious building projects. His construction of an elaborate Temple involved the quarrying of stone and the lumbering of cedar from faraway locations as well as the transportation of these materials to the Jerusalem building site. In accomplishing such an enterprise he imposed heavy personal costs on his citizens. When his son Rehoboam tries to ascend the throne and impose even greater hardships the people

---

[4] Ibid. 28–29.

[5] Hugh Pyper, "Judging the Wisdom of Solomon: The Two-Way Effect of Intertextuality," *JSOT* 59 (1993) 25–36.

[6] Ibid. 34.

rebel. They refuse to submit to the impositions, taxations, and posturing of this royal heir. A revolt by the inhabitants of the northern states leads to the division of the kingdom. Hence Solomon's proposal to divide the baby could be viewed on the surface as wise, but in the larger panorama of the unfolding biblical events the order to divide a child foreshadows the kind of wisdom that is not really wise at all. Rather, the ways of this king eventually lead to the severing of the whole nation.

Pyper, however, is not interested in critiquing kingship or monarchy *per se* as a social institution. Rather, he argues that the monarchs in both stories are examples of all human enterprise, which despite its glory is destined to fail. But the debate between these two scholars does not end here. In a subsequent article Lasine responds to Pyper's critique of his earlier work and objects to Pyper's approach.[7] Hence in these studies founded on the parallels between the women and their crises both scholars fix their analysis upon the kings and *their* crises. In complete compliance with the narrator of both tales, the debate about the character of the kings assumes center stage. In wrestling with the matter of monarchy, whether good or bad, able to succeed or destined to fail, Lasine and Pyper wrestle also with one another. The women's crises that urge interpretive attention and wrestling with the pressing issue of violence are all but eclipsed by yet another power struggle—this time an interpretive contest within the biblical guild between two scholars. The values of power and control that prevail in this biblical story echo in the pedantic rhetoric of debate across these interpretive exchanges. Yet again, in the course of these struggles, the significance of the women's stories is passed over.

The parallels between the women's stories that appeared at the heart of these studies and that instigated these two scholars' work are all but lost in the discussions. It is a real and perhaps revelatory oversight that in building a parallel kinship based on the role and stories of the women in these two tales both Lasine and Pyper have failed to recognize another parallel operative here, one involving the monarchs. In both instances when the king is confronted by these crises concerning the matter of life, each levels an order for death. Solomon commands that a sword be brought and the child be sliced in two. We can refrain from imagining what would have happened if maternal instinct had not instigated a protest. Similarly in the cannibal mothers' story, when confronted with the women's plight the king vows to behead the prophet. Again we can resist contemplating the successful fulfillment of such a promise. Instead we can pay attention to the

---

[7] Stuart Lasine, "The Ups and Downs of Monarchical Justice: Solomon and Jehoram in an Intertextual World," *JSOT* 59 (1993) 37–53.

truth that emerges in both instances. When both monarchs are confronted by controversies over life they issue orders for death. When those with power must act to avert violence among the powerless they end by leveling mandates that potentially promote further violence.

What can we make of the kinship between these two pairs of women and the accompanying parallel in the violent responses of these kings? Is there any way that dwelling on the resemblances between these women and between these kings can advance our understanding of the cannibal mothers or what is going on in this tale? Can a consideration of both sets of parallels contribute any substance to the mothers' characterization rather than only to that of the monarchs?

Earlier in our discussion we said that stories often relate to other stories and that these connections sometimes enhance our understanding. However, not all stories are written. A few years ago I sat sipping tea in the home of Rosa, a Mayan woman who told me a story. Rosa lives in the village of San Lucas Toliman, Guatemala, on the shores of Lake Atitlan. Rosa told me enthusiastically about the food cooperative and child-care cooperatives that she and the other women of the village had organized. The newly established weavers' guild was a special point of pride to her, not only because of the quality of the women's handicraft but also because of the way their own destiny and livelihood were woven into their work. After many years of devastating war and its debilitating effects upon the whole country of Guatemala this village was being restored to life by the work of these women. But as she spoke Rosa's expression of pride faded into a seriousness and concern. "This is what those with power most fear, you know," she said. "When the women of our village work together for the sake of the children, for the sake of our future, for the sake of ourselves, those who abuse power will find ways to . . ." She stopped mid-sentence, as though rehearsing the oppressive, horrific tactics of the past might somehow encourage their renewal. As I listened attentively and respectfully I began to understand what Rosa knew all too well: that women or the powerless working together in the interest of life poses an insurmountable threat to hierarchical forms of governance; that when people cooperate and live harmoniously together there is little need for hierarchical forms of power to impose control on people's lives. When people live in a more egalitarian framework bent on sharing resources and devoted to the common good and well-being of all the need for social configurations of power and control diminishes. In such circumstances self-governance replaces monarchy. People—not excessive levels of government—benefit from their own backbreaking labor. Surpluses produced in the community are reinvested back into that same community and enhance the lives of its members rather than supporting and securing a ruler's hold on his office.

Rosa's experience and story became a cultural text that exposed another connection between the two stories of two mothers before kings. In both biblical stories a subtext—that of women at odds with one another over a fundamental matter, the life of a child—coincides with and offers an evaluation of monarchy that either affirms or indicts the king and his ability to rule. How is it that stories about poor, powerless women in hostile relations with one another end up making a king look good? Solomon is proclaimed wise as the result of this story. In the other account the king tears his robe so that "the people saw the king was wearing sackcloth underneath," a gesture clearly insuring admiration and support for the monarch. Why are stories about poor, powerless women at odds with one another the occasion to spotlight the character of a king? Does the endurance of monarchy or any form of hierarchical government necessitate women remaining in conflict-ridden relationships? Is the maintenance of enmity between women essential for the maintenance of the ethos of power and domination? Or to put it another way, do poor women, or for that matter any group of classless persons working together, gravely threaten to upset and dismantle such hierarchical forms of power?

At the heart of the crises between both these pairs of women are the bankrupt institutions of patriarchal society and hierarchal governance that engender such hostilities. And these two forces are not unrelated. Patriarchy constituted the social configuration of ancient Israel. The "house of the father" *(bet 'ab)* constituted the fundamental organizing unit of society. Each person was defined by and belonged to a house governed by the father. A man's destiny, to become a father figure, was ultimately defined. A woman's lot was to remain connected to a man, first her father, then a husband as the head of another household. Rules governing individual households, religious practices, and community customs supported and reinforced this configuration. Sons rather than daughters were the recipients of their fathers' inheritance. For women to have sons was much more valued than to have daughters. Women's biological makeup was a liability and signaled their subordination in this society. During their menstrual cycle they were considered unclean. Moreover, when they birthed a female child their period of purification was longer than when they brought forth a son. If there was a question about their status as virgin after they had been bethrothed to a man, they could be stoned to death. Evidence of the subordination of women in patriarchal society is abundantly present in the biblical traditions of ancient Israel. It cuts across the religious, social, and economic practices narrated there.

However, this father-ruled society was not unrelated to the larger political structuring of this biblical world. Patriarchy does not mean only the subordination of females to males. This system of privilege and control also materialized as landholders over serfs, masters over slaves, ruling class over peasants, and kings over subjects. The patriarchal structures of the social system in Israel coincided with and corroborated the hierarchal framework of its political organization. In this stratification kings are at the top and women unattached to men are at the bottom.

Being a "wife" and a "mother" were the two opportunities whereby a woman could establish her significance and ensure herself a place in society. Moreover, in this setup motherhood had an added significance when a woman was unattached to a man. It was the only means whereby a woman could claim worth and identity. When childbearing constitutes the sole option by which a woman can define herself the crisis between two mothers over the life of a child takes on life-and-death proportions. Only in such cultural conditions could a woman who has suffered the tragedy of an infant's death be prompted to steal another mother's newborn. In such dysfunctional social frameworks children become a means to an end rather than an end in themselves. They assure integrity, acceptance, and destiny for a woman in a man's world.

In a situation where women are driven to eat their children this lack of self-worth is only further magnified. The forces creating such dehumanizing circumstances are illustrated in our tale. The war games of those with power in a hierarchical political scheme ignite a crisis within the walls of a city held hostage. Moreover, as we have seen, the struggle for power is not confined to a contest between the rulers of Israel and Aram. The wrestling for power between king and prophet also constructs a culture of conflict and competition. The women are the recipients of the fallout of such social frameworks. Subordinated by the cultural and political framework in which they reside, the women are further denigrated by consuming their only evidence of worth and identity. Eating their children, the women are alienated from their sole remaining prospect for self-worth as human beings.

These social and political forces, with their potential to destroy the capacity for good relations between persons as well as to ignite such self-destructive outcomes among the least in a society, are not confined to these two stories. The biblical text writhes with such stories of enmity and self-destruction. That the hierarchical structures and patriarchal mindsets underwrite and even instigate these hostilities between women can be verified in the following biblical tales.

## Sarah and Hagar

The story of Sarah and Hagar begins in Gen 16:1-16. Hagar is Sarah's maidservant. Sarah, who is the wife of the great patriarch Abraham, is Hagar's mistress. Hence their oppositions at the opening of the story are defined by the social configurations of this ancient hierarchal society. Additionally, we are told that Sarah is barren. Her inability to have a child will add to the opposition between these two women. Sarah's barrenness is significant both in the context of this patriarchal culture with its expectations of women and in the context of this particular family as well. As we have heard, children afforded women their worth and value in this ancient setting, and women in turn were defined by their status as wives and mothers. Hence Sarah's status as barren could be viewed as a threat to her place, status, and security in patriarchal society.

However, in this family barrenness has religious ramifications as well. God called Abraham to be the father of a great people founded on a promise of descendants "as numerous as the stars" (Gen 15:5). The realization of Abraham's destiny as well as the fulfillment of God's promise rested upon the realization of Sarah's destiny and the fulfillment of her role as mother in that setting. Hence Sarah's barrenness joins both social and theological significance and consequences. Sarah's response to her circumstances might suggest the urgency of such a crisis in this patriarchal household. Deciding in favor of what was an apparently acceptable practice, she gives Hagar, her maidservant, to Abraham in hope of conception by proxy. In her role as surrogate mother, Hagar conceives. But immediately this new life occasions enmity between the women. Once she is with child, Hagar disregards Sarah. "When she saw that she had conceived, she looked with contempt on her mistress" (16:4). In turn Sarah's own jealously prompts her to mistreat Hagar. "Then Sarah dealt harshly with her, and she ran away from her" (16:6).

Hagar deserts her mistress and escapes to the wilderness. Here she is met by an angel of God who urges her to "return and submit" to Sarah (16:9). However, an unprecedented annunciation along with a promise accompany this coaxing. Hagar is told she has conceived a son whom she will call Ishmael. Additionally, her encounter includes a promise that her descendants will also become numerous. The first part of the story then comes to a conclusion with a report of Ishmael's birth.

When the story reopens in Gen 21:1-21 Hagar has apparently returned to Sarah, but a great deal more has also happened that would seem to bring an end to the opposition between them. In the intervening chapters God promised Sarah that despite her old age she would have a son (Genesis 19). Now, as the chapter opens, we hear that what has been promised has been fulfilled. Sarah has given birth to Isaac. But as the story continues, so also does the strife between the two women.

Abraham holds a banquet on the occasion of the weaning of Isaac, his son. Upon seeing the two children, Isaac and Ishmael, playing together, Sarah fears that her son's claim on Abraham's inheritance will be compromised. The potential negative consequences for herself and her child are sufficient for Sarah to take action. Immediately she urges Abraham to cast out the mother and child from their household. Though reluctant, Abraham dismisses Hagar with her son Ishmael and sends them into the dangerous wilderness. Wandering in this life-threatening, barren place, Hagar finally places her crying son under a bush to die. She sits down at a distance as if to shield herself from his final moments of wailing while at the same time still watching over him in her role as a mother.

Once again God responds to her desperate circumstances, as well as to the weeping child. Hagar is instructed to pick up the child and hold him safe. At the same moment God shows her a spring and provides water for them. The story ends with the summary narrating that their crisis was resolved. The boy grew up in the wilderness and eventually married a woman chosen by his mother from the Egyptians. Thus not only did the son have life, but life was assured for his mother as well.

In contrast to the story of the two harlots before the king, the links between Sarah and Hagar's story and that of the tale of the two cannibal mothers seem less clear at first glance. Sarah and Hagar were struggling over what seemed to be a matter of social and personal import—the matter of conception and birth of a child. The cannibal mothers' struggle was about a more pressing, immediate, and fundamental condition—physical starvation and the threat to the life of the remaining child. An expression of contempt on Hagar's part when she became pregnant and Sarah's jealous response to this successful conception fueled their controversy. By contrast, we hear nothing of the feelings or emotions of the cannibal mothers. No expression of jealousy, contempt, sadness, or even hatred animates their feeling life. Yet this absence of parallel between the two pairs of women may itself be revelatory. To survive by eating one's offspring, one has had to become detached from all feeling. The conditions of famine in Samaria have not only created the physical circumstances of severe hunger; extreme food stress in a milieu of oppression urges persons to hoard food, steal from one another, and commit crimes against one another in the pursuit of survival.[8] If these conditions persist, a person is gradually stripped

---

[8] See the discussion of the correlation between oppressive societies and the incidence of cannibalism in times of food stress in Chapter 4 above.

of her feeling life as a human being. In contrast to Sarah and Hagar, the cannibal mothers' controversy is not fueled by feeling. Unlike the harlot mother who burned with compassion for her son before Solomon, the cannibal mothers give no indication of emotion. Appropriately, no narrative report of sorrow, remorse, revulsion, or even anger animates these women. Plundered of all that makes them human, they have lost even their maternal instinct. Reduced to raw appetite as explanation for their deeds, they are numb!

Still, there are connections to be made with the Sarah and Hagar story—connections whereby the cannibal mothers' status as social equals informs our reading of this Genesis tale. At first glance the controversy between Sarah and Hagar appears in different terms than the struggle between the mothers. Sarah is a mistress. Hagar is her maidservant. The social stratification that makes them unequals encourages their controversy.

The narrative surrounding them even engenders this inequity. A significantly larger portion of narrative is devoted to developing Sarah's character. We first encounter her in a genealogy (Gen 11:29), where she is introduced as "Sarai, wife of Abram." Characteristically such litanies were devoted to recording men's names in a patriarchal society. Here Abraham's father, Terah, and his descendants are recorded. As these ancestral narratives unfold we hear of several references to Sarah's physical beauty. Abraham himself proclaims, "I know well that you are a woman beautiful in appearance . . ." (Gen 12:11). In fact, on account of her beauty he often fears for his life. Because of her attractiveness, while they are in a foreign court he urges her to say that she is his sister (Gen 12:11). When they are in Egypt, the Egyptians tell Pharaoh of her beauty. Pharaoh himself, as well as his princes, praises her for her fair appearance (Gen 12:14, 15). Abraham even benefits because of her "good looks." But the casting of Sarah's character is not limited to narrative description. Unlike many women in the Bible, Sarah also speaks and acts. She speaks with Abraham and even decides what will happen to Hagar. In the larger narrative she has identity as the first mother in Israel, the wife of Abraham, the bearer of an ancestral heir, Isaac.

In concert with the narrative depiction of Hagar as maidservant of Sarah, the narrative description reinforces Hagar's secondary status. Little is offered about Hagar in the story line. She is identified as Egyptian, yet as with the cannibal mothers we have no description of what she looks like or anything else about her. That neither Abraham nor Sarah refers to her by her name reduces her visibility further. In the company of Sarah she never speaks, and while she is spoken about by Abraham and Sarah, they never speak directly to her. Others decide what will happen to her. She is never consulted. As maidservant she is adjunct to Sarah's character. The lack of narrative description reinforces her social role as underling.

However, when set alongside the story of the cannibal mothers this depiction of Sarah and Hagar as different and unequal may not be as real as it seems. In the story of the cannibal mothers we have no evidence of difference or inequality between the women. Whether there ever was any social stratification, we do not know. What we do know is the impact oppression has upon the status of human persons in relation to one another. When persons are subjugated and stripped of their humanity all that makes them different or even unequal is gone. There is no hint of inequality between the cannibal mothers. Moreover, the violence and oppression that renders them victims of the power plays of a monarch and prophet make both women equally victims, regardless of their previous state.

Similarly, while the narrative sketches characterizations that create differences as well as inequalities between Sarah and Hagar, these distinctions are mere facades. While she is apparently the one with power over her maidservant, Sarah's own identity and self-worth are under siege in these patriarchal environs. Threatened and diminished by the expectations of this social framework, Sarah is also powerless and subjugated. Though she is powerless in her role as maidservant, Hagar's ability to conceive renders her powerful. As successful surrogate mother with child she threatens to have more stature than Sarah in this deriding context. Hence the subjugations of both classism and gender roles in the patriarchal environs render either woman powerful or powerless depending upon her capacity to conceive a child. In the end these conditions of oppression and subjugation show these women to be more alike than they are different. That God responds to both Hagar and Sarah further levels the playing field between them. Sarah—who remains within the patriarchal setting—is granted a son, which affords her identity and destiny. Hagar—who is banished to the wilderness—is given care and livelihood there. Moreover, it is significant to note that once in the wilderness, outside the bonds of patriarchal culture, Hagar is a different character. She is free from the constraints on women of the patriarchal society. She is liberated from the struggle with Sarah. Only in the wilderness, outside the social configurations of classism and hierarchy, do we hear her voice and see her character. Here she prays to God, weeps over her child, and even receives a divine promise parallel to the promise made to Abraham. In this place devoid of the structures of patriarchy the woman's voice is audible and God's voice to a woman is heard.

## Rachel and Leah

In a patriarchal world opposition often defines the relations between nations. It can also delineate the bonds between persons of the same nation. But the potential of this infectious force to seed and nurture hostilities knows no limits. It can overlay the interaction between neighbors. It can even extend its sting to members of the same family. Rachel and Leah are sisters, but the patriarchal milieu of their story occasions a tale of contest and rivalry between them. As sisters they are daughters of the same mother and father. As rivals they are wives of the same husband, Jacob. But this polygamous arrangement, a familiar convention in the ancient world, does not explain their hostility. Like the crisis at the heart of the loathing between Hagar and Sarah, the matter of barrenness instigates this relationship of rivalry. But unlike the mistress and her slave woman, Rachel and Leah are equals, related by birth and by blood. Introduced as siblings, they become opponents. While their stories are told as one, the unfolding tale separates them. Moreover, it is a story at the service of a larger tale, the story of the man Jacob.

At the urging of his mother Rebekkah, and with the blessing of his father Isaac, Jacob is journeying to find a wife in the land of his uncle Laban, his mother's brother. Rachel and Leah's story (Genesis 29–35) begins when Jacob enters the land of his relatives. Upon arriving, he first encounters Rachel (29:6). Seeing her coming with her father's flocks, he rolls the stone away from the mouth of a well and waters her sheep. He greets her with a kiss and is so overjoyed that he bursts into tears.

Rachel runs to announce his arrival to her parents. Jacob follows, meets his uncle, and agrees to stay and work for him. Laban asks what Jacob will exact of him in exchange for his labor. Momentarily the narrative account of these negotiations pauses and we are offered a parenthetical aside (29:16-17). This brief interruption informs us that Laban has two daughters. Though our introduction to them is scant, it sets up a contrast between them. First Leah is introduced. The description is abbreviated and unclear. She is older *(gedolah)* and the accompanying description of her eyes is difficult to translate. Some render the Hebrew "there was no sparkle in Leah's eyes." Others translate "her eyes were lovely." Hence a question mark hovers over what little we know of Leah's appearance (29:17). By contrast, Rachel is identified as younger. In appearance she is "beautiful." When she moves she is "graceful." So attractive is she that Jacob falls immediately in love with her. This brief narrative detour concludes as abruptly as it began and the focus on Jacob's story continues.

Jacob agrees to work seven years for Laban in order to have Rachel's hand in marriage. When Jacob has completed his side of this "work in exchange for a woman" bargain the wedding banquet is planned, and Jacob expects to be given his future wife Rachel. However, Laban has a change of heart and defaults on his side of the bargain. In place of Rachel "he takes" and "brings" Leah, incognito, to Jacob in the night. But it takes Jacob until morning to discover that he has been tricked by Laban. When the disconcerted Jacob confronts his uncle, Laban agrees to give Rachel to Jacob on the condition that he is willing to work seven more years for him. This second agreement of "work in exchange for a woman" makes clear the status of women as commodities in patriarchal society. Whether it is the dowry a father pays a would-be husband for his daughter or the number of years a man labors, women have a pricetag attached to them.

When Jacob agrees to this new bargain, Laban provides his other daughter as a second wife to Jacob. Immediately he sleeps with her, and the narrator observes that Jacob loved Rachel more than Leah. Once again the machinations of men, both those in the story and those who tell the story, seed enmity between women. First, at the level of story, Jacob's favorable response to one woman diminishes the other and thus encourages enmity. Next, at the level of narration, the uneven and contrasting characterization of these sisters paves the way for the opposition that will surface between them. Though these differences are minimal, they narrate the oppositions.

Rachel is active. She is introduced first in the narrative when Jacob enters the land. She sees, she runs, and she has a voice. She is a messenger to her parents. She is spoken to and is the recipient of kisses. The center of men's attentions and affections, she turns heads. Though she is the second daughter, the narrative description elevates her above the first-born. Leah, by contrast, is passive. She merits only the brief description as "older" *(gedolah)*, with eyes of ambiguous description. She functions as Laban's instrument to deceive Jacob. On her wedding night she has no voice. In the darkness of night and of Laban's deed she has no face. When Jacob comes to her in the night she has no choice. Though she, too, is introduced as an actor in the story, she is only acted upon.

Though joined to the same husband, Rachel and Leah are alienated as sisters and as characters. Their opposition is further exaggerated by what follows. Rachel, who is loved by Jacob, is barren. Leah, the less favored, is not. This contrasting capacity to bear children complicates their characterization and further aggravates their relationship. A frenzy of births follows, fueling the competition. The litany-like account of this activity oscillates back and forth, suggesting score-keeping in a high-stakes competition (29:31-35). First Leah conceives four times and gives birth to four sons while Rachel remains barren. Then Rachel takes matters into her own hands. Like Sarah, she solves the problem by giving her servant woman,

Bilhah, to Jacob. Bilhah conceives twice and bears two sons for Rachel. Leah matches Rachel's ingenuity. She also takes and gives her servant woman, Zilpah, to Jacob, and Zilpah conceives and bears two sons.

Next we hear that Leah's son is returning from the field with mandrakes for his mother. While the significance of this report is not immediately clear to a contemporary reader, studies suggest that in the ancient world mandrakes were thought to be of value in promoting fertility.[9] Immediately Rachel pleads with Leah for some of the mandrakes. Leah agrees, but with one caveat. In exchange for some of the potent plants Leah claims nuptial time with Jacob that night. However, her husband evidently comes to her more than just that one evening. The narrative that follows records that Leah conceives and gives birth three more times, first to two sons and then to one daughter. Finally, amidst this frenetic tournament of birth for birth, "God remembered Rachel" and she conceives and gives birth to a son (33:22).

Here, birthing of children reveals itself in the baldest of terms as a contest between women for self-worth and identity. Leah seeks children in order to secure the love and affection of her husband. When her first son is born she exclaims, "Now my husband will love me" (29:32). Similarly, Rachel's desperate longing for children secures her own self-worth. Her only recorded response to her sister's birthings is jealousy. "When Rachel saw that she bore Jacob no children, she envied her sister" (30:1). In turn Rachel issues a desperate ultimatum to Jacob, "Give me children, or I shall die" (30:2).

Rachel and Leah's efforts unfold as a desperate contest to have children, but the story also discloses more. As the narrative report seesaws back and forth the women vie for a husband's affection and favor. Their own self-worth is at stake. Their future and security hinge upon the destiny that progeny ensures.

As wives of the same husband Rachel and Leah are pawns in a patriarchal story and a patriarchal society. Like the other women's stories, the tale of these sisters and their strife is of no particular account except as it contributes to a larger tale. The opposition that divides them contributes to this tale. Dwarfed by the tradition and the history of the patriarch, the women's story is adjunct. Like Sarah and Hagar, the inequality between the women is complicated. While Rachel is beautiful, she is also barren. And though Leah's appearance is more ambiguous, she bears six sons. Hence the ignominy of the opposition seeded by this kind of milieu is wearisome here. The hierarchical nature of patriarchal society that meas-

---

[9] Gordon Wenham, *Genesis 16–50*. WBC 2 (Waco: Word Books, 1994) 246.

ures one person as more worthy than another shows its repulsive tenacity. Standards of what is beautiful in men's eyes encourage stratifications between persons. The capacity to bear children as provision of a man's legacy and pleasure reinforces further gradations. Grounded in the promotion of competition and rivalry, patriarchy demonstrates in this story the depth of its influence. It fuels opposition even between sisters.

When Rachel and Leah's story is set alongside the story of the two cannibal mothers there are parallel features as well as great irony. In both stories the pairs of women are at odds with one another, prompted by the circumstances of patriarchy and the related hierarchical society. Like Rachel and Leah's, the cannibal mothers' destinies depend on the response of a man. Jacob, we have noted, is more than willing to attend to the well-being of both his wives. He provides children through them and even through their women servants. Similarly, a man also figures in the progression of the story of the cannibal mothers. The king, the penultimate image of power in patriarchal society, appears as the potential source of hope and life for these women in their desperate straits. However, the man with the most power appears embarrassingly powerless. Moreover, his lack of power matches his lack of integrity. In addition to blaming God for women's poverty and starvation, he is utterly unresponsive to their immediate need for food. Thus the cannibal mothers vie for the one child remaining between them.

While one woman wants the child for food, the motivation of the other mother who hides it is unclear. That she has had a change of heart prompted by maternal compassion is possible. However, it is also likely that in these desperate straits she is keeping him all for herself and her own sustenance. The narrative does not tell, but the alienation of these women from their socialized role as mothers is guaranteed. As Rachel and Leah struggle to ascertain self-worth and destiny, the struggle of the cannibal mothers leads to the surrender of self-worth and destiny. In fact, Rachel and Leah explicitly make clear that children are their links to meaning and self-worth. However, in the case of the cannibal mothers, the horror of consuming their children competes with the horror of all that is lost in such an act. Eating their own children estranges them from their posture as mothers. Hence they are robbed of identity. Not only do their children die, but so do their own destinies and self-worth. Consumption of their children constitutes their own self-destruction. That the poetics of their story make them faceless concurs with this outcome and even emphasizes it.

On the surface the contrast in the strife between sisters and between mothers seems clear. While the two sisters are in a desperate competition to have children, the two cannibal mothers are at odds with one another over the consumption of the remaining child. But taken together their stories reveal more about our two characters. For the cannibal mothers, alienation eclipses their struggle with each other. Plumbing the depths of this riveting contrast illuminates the diminishing options each has for self-definition as well as the alienation of each mother from herself. Their namelessness corroborates such straits and foreshadows the utter loss of self.

The antics that configure both patriarchal society and monarchical governance are not limited to sowing enmity between the powerless in society, however. This condition is but a part of a larger and more pervasive scheme. Vertical violence is at work here as well. A monarch imposes demands on the royal class who in turn transfer these demands down upon their charges. In turn these persons who are commissioned with overseeing the laboring class shift the mounting burdens upon them. In the course of these social gradations the use and abuse of power shifts from one class to the next, and with it the concomitant violence passes along from one social level to the next until it infects the whole social framework. As this discord and abuse descends, it weighs heaviest upon the least in a society. In serpentine fashion violence mutates and duplicates itself. Unchecked, this vertical violence at the lowest levels of stratified society gives way to horizontal violence. Among the least of a society—among women, day laborers, peasants—violence infects the bonds of relationship between them.

As it is for Sarah and Hagar, the two prostitute mothers before Solomon, Rachel and Leah, and the cannibal mothers, the opposition between women is tied to the matters of life. The cannibal mothers and the women before Solomon struggle over the life of a living child. Sarah and Hagar as well as Rachel and Leah are set at odds over their capacities for childbirth. The oppositions that erupt across these classes of women in patriarchal culture know no boundaries. Nameless women, harlots, elite women, maidservants, and even sisters all are victims in the vertical violence of patriarchy.

The oppositions and the hostilities they breed are difficult to curtail. They spread and extend to oppress others in their path. In the story of Rachel and Leah the hostility between sisters turns to further vicitimization. As slave women of these sisters, Zilpah and Bilhah are enlisted to participate in this unofficial contest. While they have names, they seem not to have a choice. They are required to sleep with a man, conceive, and bear children for someone else. The children of their wombs become the children of another. The children of their wombs give identity to another. The children of their wombs become the legacy of another. They are only present in the story and in this patriarchal family to serve the needs and interests of another. However, at the same time oppression has a way of leveling the playing field. Though Rachel and Leah are their mistresses, these four women are united in their status as the subjugated. All four serve the interests and the needs of another, Jacob.

Similarly, the struggle between the cannibal mothers extends its hostilities beyond their opposition. The life of one child has been snuffed out. The life of another child in the wings is threatened. Unchecked, the hostilities between persons always lead to further oppressions and subjugations. The oppression of these women in a patriarchal society, a society of war games and elitist contests, leads to their oppression of their own children. The cannibalizing of the children leaves the mothers without identity, worth, or value in the society and thus ensnares them in a further round of oppression and loss.

## Conclusion

The stories of each of these pairs of women put them at odds with one another. The parallels and contrasts that have emerged above illuminate further the meager information we have in building the character of these cannibal mothers. However, when we situate all three of these other accounts together alongside the story of our cannibal mothers some even more staggering insights brand their mark on our consciousnesses.

While all three pairs of women—the two harlot women before Solomon, Sarah and Hagar, and Rachel and Leah—tell stories of conflict, all three achieve resolution. While all three of these tales serve the interests of or are subordinate to a larger story that is not theirs, each story ultimately comes to a conclusion.

Sarah and Hagar's account participates in building the legacy and story of Abraham. Still, their struggle with one another finds a settlement that attends to both of their interests. God grants barren Sarah a son, Isaac, and thus provides her an heir and fulfillment of her place in that society. Though banished to the wilderness, Hagar and her son are provided protection and longevity. In addition, they are the unexpected recipients of a divine promise that parallels God's promise to Abraham. They will have numerous descendants and become a great nation.

The crisis of the two harlot women before Solomon is addressed. Though also nameless and lacking attachments to men, their complaint receives attention and action from the king. Without a doubt their story is told to illuminate the wisdom and greatness of the monarch. Still, the gravity of their crisis warrants attention and resolution. In the process the infant's true mother is identified. With the child's return to its true mother the conflict dissipates. In the end a further tragedy resulting from the crisis of one woman's loss of her infant is curtailed.

In the story of Rachel and Leah the enmity between sisters also plays a part in the larger story of Jacob. Still, within the confines of the story of the patriarch the women's crisis achieves a settlement. Both women long for children. We heard that Leah seeks offspring as instruments for securing her husband's affection and love, and she bears sons and a daughter. Rachel, who longs for children as a means of livelihood and self-worth, is also satisfied. Though at first the patriarch Jacob himself in not able to grant Rachel's request, God steps in and resolves her barrenness.

While we have noted previously that the cannibal mothers' difficulty goes unaddressed, the outcomes and resolutions in these other three stories further aggravate this circumstance. Not only is the cannibal mothers' conflict left unresolved, but the life of an infant hangs in the balance. Moreover, as we have noted, the king never responds to the starvation of the women. Even though his act of fasting in the face of these starving women hints that he has access to food, they are left to eat their own children. However, though other prospects for the resolution of their food crisis are lodged in the surrounding narrative, they are never realized. Indeed, the story indicates that though prices are outrageous in the marketplace there is some food to be had by those who can still afford it. That the women decide to eat their own children suggests that the economics of this social situation bar them from access to even this sustenance.

So while there is some indication of food still available, there is no hint of provision made in response to these women. As their story goes unresolved, so also does their crisis—both their conflict and their starvation. Moreover, the story gives no hint of God stepping in. Unlike the women in our other stories, the cannibal mothers receive no response from the most powerful figures in the biblical tradition. Neither God nor the king intervenes. Instead, the mothers are left to die.

These nameless, blameless victims are but signs of a world gone horribly awry. Human sentiment has lost touch with its heart and its ability to respond empathetically. Its feeling life has become bankrupt. These mothers and their tale become the commentary for how far this violence of classism, patriarchy, and political hegemony has advanced. Moreover, their tale becomes a diagnostic test for readers of just how contagious this cancerous growth really is.

Does their crisis merely prompt dismissive revulsion, or does it occasion head-shaking incredulity? Does their story incite only condemnation, or does it provoke tears? Does their unbelievable circumstance incite disregard and disqualification, or does it ignite outrage and galvanize one's determination to act on behalf of such victims?

As part of a literary work the development of these mothers and their story demonstrates the fullness and import that even minor characters can achieve. As characters in a religious text of the Bible these mothers evoke much more. Though nameless and faceless, they challenge us to grapple with the problems of systemic violence threaded across the story of salvation history and on down into our own lives. We see that some of the structures that lead to their victimization are recognizable in our own time. Additionally, these women sensitize us to the complexity of even identifying the forms and dynamics of violence in our quest to resist these currents. Their story helps us understand that the sentiments compelling humans' disregard for one another go deep. They are not only embedded in the visible structures of social and political frameworks; they are etched within the human psyche itself. Hence our study of these mothers does invite us to continue building character . . . but this time to build our own.

The cannibal mothers' story mandates the shattering of frameworks that would prevent us from recognizing their plight. This close look at their characters demands the dismantling of social configurations that allow us to excuse ourselves from responsibility, to blame someone else, or even worse, not even to respond. Finally, their characters cry out for something more. They beseech us to overturn their story. They call upon us to embrace their counterparts in our own world—persons whose emaciated lives are similarly being swallowed up in the jaws of war, impoverishment, and non-identity.

# CHAPTER SIX

*Character, Counter Texts, and Conclusion*

What began as a study of minor characters turns out to be a not so minor study. Training our attention on the two cannibal mothers has revealed more than a passing tale about two insignificant characters. Though their story appears overshadowed by the more commanding tale of king and prophet, what we have discovered cannot easily be dismissed. In the course of the investigation our determination to dwell upon the mothers as characters and what they might reveal has harvested an abundance of disquieting insights and compelling challenges. That these women and their life-threatening circumstances are never addressed is quite disturbing. That one infant's livelihood is left under threat incites horror and disbelief. Even more, that the whole history of biblical interpretation has either ignored them or condemned them all together merits condemnation itself.

We began with what appeared to be a rather insignificant though perhaps repulsive little story about two women groveling for survival by quarreling over one child as food. However, as we resisted the narrator's attention on the king and the prophet and inquired further about these seemingly insignificant characters we discovered how their own destinies were being cut off by the misdeeds of those with power. In addition, as this brief story was allowed time to interact with the other tales—the account of the two harlot women before Solomon (1 Kings 3:16-28), the tradition of Sarah and Hagar (Genesis 16; 21), and the tale of Rachel and Leah (Genesis 29–31)—the parallels, connections, and even contrasts that ricocheted between these accounts exposed the violence of the hierarchical systems of both patriarchy and monarchy in which these stories were grounded. Moreover, how the oppressive classism of both patriarchy and monarchy reinforces the scaffolding of this ruthless infrastructure has also been revealed. Monarchic forms of government and patriarchal arrangements of society are underwritten by the same bottom line. They both rest on large numbers of nameless, lower class, and powerless persons situated in a dependent relation to those with power. More often than not these relations of dependence work to the advantage of those with power by sowing the seeds of abusive behaviors toward the powerless as well as among the powerless. The powerless assimilate the values and behavior of their oppressors. In turn, abusive behavior becomes endemic among the powerless. In a society where the maintenance of political and social order is founded on abusive power over others the violence becomes systemic. The endurance of those in power is ensured if hostility defines the relations among the powerless. Violence among the powerless helps to keep them without power and succeeds in perpetuating the need for hierarchy. Hence it is not only inevitable but also essential that such groups of dependent individuals be infected with the same violence that afflicts them.

In this regard stories about opposition between such persons serve not only as symptoms but also as consequences of this violent system. Additionally, they serve as reinforcement of this deadly framework. Systemic violence becomes endemic. As we have seen, the story of our two cannibal mothers is a case in point. However, this dynamic is not easily recognized when such a story is read in isolation. Only when it is repositioned alongside similar stories and read in concert with them does the intrinsic and repetitive nature of the violence underwriting both patriarchy and monarchy make itself known. Indeed, such an interpretation of a biblical story is disquieting. Earlier we said that this character building enterprise was not confined to the characters in the text. As we study these persons closely, and work for understanding and meaning, character may also be built in us. Character building happens in us when we gain insight, grow in understanding, become more compassionate, and rise to new challenges. These characters in our biblical tale level a challenge and offer insights, but we must wrestle with the challenge to gain these insights. The challenge set forth is the problem of violence and how to respond to it. Here the violence is confined to the story world of these two mothers, but we recognize it because of our own familiarity with violence in our own world. What response can we make to this and other similar stories we claim as our sacred tradition? Can the way we read texts begin to confront and overpower this debilitating force?

## Strategies for Reading Violent Texts[1]

Some have found it acceptable to ignore such stories as the cannibal mothers and bypass the violence associated with them. Indeed, avoidance would be a possible response if we lived in a peaceful world where such stories were of no consequence. However, that is not the case in our own time. We know the violence of war, of terrorism, and of an impoverished two-thirds world. We know the violence of powerless people left landless and the violence resorted to by the powerful whose land holdings are threatened. Even the more subtle forms of violence—bigotry, ignorance, prejudice—constantly rear their heads in our era. No, our world is not placid, nonviolent, or unilaterally committed to peace. A decision to look the other way or to gloss over occasions of violence in such tales as the cannibal mothers, or in any stories of our sacred canon, is not an option. A decision for complacency can have fateful consequences. Whether in our lives or in these texts, a decision to ignore acts of cruelty or savagery becomes complicity with such deeds and only serves to breed further violence.

The current state of our world mandates that we cannot afford to be naïve or shortsighted when we encounter violence, especially in the biblical tradition. Across human history these stories and their interpretations have had life-and-death consequences. From the Crusades to World War II, from the Inquisition to the Holocaust, from witch hunts to Palestinian Refugee Camps in the West Bank the biblical texts have been called upon to justify war, endorse slavery, support prejudices, persecute the innocent, and degrade women. The Bible and our interpretation of its traditions *does* matter. It shapes and justifies responses made by the state. It grounds and informs the belief system of the Church. And more often than not ordinary people turn to the biblical texts for inspiration as they grapple with particular social realities in the past or with the global challenges of our own time.

As our study of the cannibal mothers has taught us, we would be shortsighted and even delinquent if we adopted easy solutions to the problems of violence in the biblical traditions. The development of our own character depends on our willingness to wrestle with these problems and to do the hard work involved in negotiating such texts. Four strategies are proposed here as points of departure.

First, we can draw upon the helpful investigations of social science studies of traditions to inform our readings. We must do so in the most comprehensive way possible. For example, we discovered that it is not sufficient to focus solely upon an investigation of the office and responsibilities

---

[1] In an earlier article I have discussed some of these strategies. See "Violence in Joshua and Judges," *The Bible Today* 39 (July 2001) 196–203.

of the king in our story. Nor is it enough to attend to understanding the task of a prophet and the development of this role in Israelite society. We saw how inquiring about cannibalism and its accompanying social and political conditions alters first impressions of this story and its characters. Most significantly, it shifted the indictment away from the starving women and pointed a finger at the king. Our social science investigation of cannibalism not only argued for the helplessness of the women in this socio-political situation but also revealed that an oppressive system of monarchy was the real cannibalizing culprit. Lives, destinies, identities, and well-being were being swallowed up in power-hungry monarchical machinations. Such understandings do not endorse or erase the violence in this account, but they serve at least to qualify what we read here. Hence social science investigations of all aspects and characters are an important prelude to addressing violence in texts.

Second, we can read the stories of annihilation, brutality, and degradation of such characters as the cannibal mothers *in memoriam*. Recognition, reflection, and remembrance of victims in our own sacred traditions not only reinstates the dignity often lost to them in the history of interpretation; it might also be one way we can begin to identify those who suffer violence in our own world. Our Jewish brothers and sisters are an example in this regard. Every year during the Seder meal at Passover they remember the Egyptians who, according to the biblical tradition, were slaughtered as a result of Israel's liberation from bondage.

Across our biblical traditions numerous nameless, faceless persons are conscripted as background for the story world. Often the victims of oppression and violence, they are easily lost in the reading and recitation of our sacred traditions. The story that tells of the construction of Solomon's elaborate Temple and palace only mentions in passing the many thousands of laborers who were conscripted into backbreaking service in the realization of this king's architectural ambitions. When Josiah, a king of Judah, initiated a religious reform to centralize cult and worship in Jerusalem he received great praise. Referenced only indirectly in the account of his great accomplishment are the scores of unnamed men and women working at local shrines who lost their jobs as a result of this king's "religious" fervor. With great zeal the narrative in Joshua and Judges recalls the comprehensive destruction Israel accomplished when it came into the land of Canaan. The narrative only implies the immense numbers of innocent Canaanite people dwelling in their homes when Israel accomplished its conquest of Canaan by mass destruction. The biblical tradition teems with hints about or explicit evidence of victims who all too often bear the burden of a story in which they receive no attention or mention. Nameless, they are often the "extras" in the background who bear a perilous resemblance to our cannibal mothers and such persons in our own time. Like their literary counterparts, our contemporaries too have suffered violence at others' expense or instigation but are also comprehensively ignored.

Third, we must read in a fashion that documents the case against violence and its perpetrators. Attention to the varieties of brutality in the biblical texts cultivates our own sensitivity to violence in all its forms. No one would fail to recognize that the murder, seizure of property, and rape played out across the stories in the Bible are acts of violence. However, there are other forms of annihilation in these texts that must also be acknowledged in order to be uprooted. Our study of the cannibal mothers has demonstrated this. Recognizing such textual violence often requires that we become resistant readers. We must resist reading with the narrator and letting the storyteller decide which characters to feature. We also may have to resist our own tendency to identify with the major characters, those with the most power, honor, or attention. We need to inquire whether a story is told at someone's expense. We need to consider whether a story has a debilitating effect on some social group beyond the text. We need to be mindful of whether the story serves to reinforce hostility toward some group over and against another. The process of reading itself can quell or cultivate violence. It can be an act of oppression or it can be an act of resistance.

In all this we have to resist hurrying to an interpretation about what, on the surface, looks like an innocent tale. Reading and interpretation as well as composition can be acts of violence. The namelessness that encumbers some characters and the blame that some will shoulder in a story can be more than interesting and innocent literary gestures. The opportunity for speech denied to some characters, the designation of some women and men as expendable, and the lack of social standing given to such characters as virgin daughters, widows, and women in general—all these are subtle but nevertheless real examples of violence in these accounts. If we fail to recognize and decry the more indirect, though still dehumanizing forms of brutality in biblical traditions, we will most likely miss them in our own lives as well.

Fourth, we must search and read counter texts alongside such stories as our cannibal mothers. Counter texts are stories that participate in the same encumbering contexts—patriarchy and hierarchy—that produce victims and violence in other tales, yet yield different conclusions. They narrate a story line that resists these violent currents. They set forth characters who seem able to break out of oppressive cultural encumbrances and habits of relationships. They demonstrate what can happen when persons refuse violence. They are stories that fashion an alternative to such tales as our cannibal mothers. In this regard they might demonstrate the possibilities that arise when minor characters are emboldened to reject the game plan of monarchal authority. They may demonstrate the freedom of characters who reside on the fringes or outside of patriarchal constraints. Moreover, as counter story to the texts we have considered, they might dramatize the incredible outcome that is possible when those without power work together in the interest of life. In countering our tale of the cannibal mothers a counter text would still call on us to pay attention to minor characters, but unlike those in our story, the counter story's characters would find a way to move beyond the constraints and patterns of violence that so encumbered their counterparts in other tales. Instead, as their story unfolded we would not only witness a story line that was alterative to other story lines and liberative for these characters: we would also be put on a trajectory of empowerment leading toward transformation of our own world.

## A Counter Text

The story in Exod 1:8–2:10 crafts such a tale. It unfolds in two parts at the opening of this second book of the canon.[2] Part 1 (1:8-21) narrates the crisis of the Hebrew people enslaved by the Pharaoh of Egypt. It opens with the notation that "a new king arose over Egypt, who did not know Joseph" (1:8). Joseph was one of the twelve sons of Jacob who had risen to the status of viceroy in Egypt (Gen 41:39-45). During a period of great famine in Canaan, Joseph is a means to life and livelihood for his father and brothers and their families. Under Joseph's care they leave their lives in Canaan and resettle in Egypt. Here Joseph provides the link to well-being in a foreign land. However, the opening of our story in Exodus suggests that all this has been forgotten. Crisis is introduced at the opening of the story when a new Pharaoh arises who has no ties or allegiances to Joseph's family and their descendants. Everything changes for this extended Hebrew family. They who had once found refuge in a foreign land and had become numerous and flourished are now enslaved by the Egyptians. Conscripted to backbreaking labor, they are the backbone of a flourishing Egyptian metropolis. And as their numbers increase, so also do their burdens. Still, as our story unfolds, they apparently pose a threat to the Egyptian Pharaoh.

---

[2] Years ago J. Cheryl Exum set forth a literary assessment of this tale disclosing that the liberation of Israel from Egyptian bondage was founded upon the refusal of women to cooperate with oppression. Cf. J. Cheryl Exum, "'You Shall Let Every Daughter Live': A Study of Exodus 1:8–2:10," *Semeia* 28 (1983) 63–82.

In part 2 (2:1-10) the camera zooms in on one Hebrew family and what actions they take in dealing with the tyrannical policies of this new ruler. As the introduction to this closeup segment begins we are immediately aware that once again the definition of this family's identity in terms of the house of the father *(bet 'ab)* signifies the existence of the larger patriarchal system in which it participates. This second part is introduced with "Now a man from the house of Levi went and married a Levite woman" (2:1). Levi was one of the twelve sons of Jacob who had come down to Egypt. Even though the second part of the larger story will primarily feature women as the main players in this segment—the mother of a baby, the baby's sister, the Pharaoh's daughter, and her maidservants—the introduction establishes its patriarchal moorings. It opens by anchoring what soon unfolds by means of women to the identification of a man's house, the house of Levi. Hence at the very beginning of both parts of our story we are immediately alerted to both the hierarchal configuration of government, which so far we have seen to have negative consequences for the powerless, and the perdurance of patriarchy, a frequent accomplice of hierarchal forms of government.

As we transition from Genesis to Exodus we anticipate that here the second part of God's promise to the Israelites is about to be fulfilled. God had promised Abraham and Sarah land and descendants (Gen 17:2-8). Descendants were a welcomed gift in the ancient world. In that time and place, where rates of infant mortality and disease were high, the prospect of descendants "as numerous as the stars" would truly require an act of God. Hence stories like those of Sarah and Hagar and Rachel and Leah narrated the tension around both the prospect of and the threat to the fulfillment of this divine scheme. Across the stories of this first biblical book the families of Abraham and Sarah, Isaac and Rebekah, and Jacob, Rachel, and Leah unfolded. Eventually a legacy of descendants as promised by God more than materialized. At the end of Genesis, Jacob and his eleven sons moved south to Egypt to avoid the famine in their land. There, with their brother Joseph as a member of Pharaoh's cabinet, they had hoped to find sustenance and life. Hence as the book of Exodus opens we anticipate the second part of God's promise being fulfilled.

The promise that still awaits fulfillment is that of land. Across Genesis the ancestors never ascend to ownership of any land. The one reference to land possession comes when Abraham is granted a cave in the field of Machpelah opposite Mamre to bury his wife Sarah (Genesis 23). Though the hope for the long-anticipated land is reiterated several times across Exodus in the most alluring of terms, "a land flowing with milk and honey" (Exod 3:8), fulfillment of the promise of land lies beyond even this book.

As the years passed and new generations awaited the fulfillment of God's promise, a new Pharaoh arose in Egypt "who did not know Joseph" (Exod 1:8). Gradually Jacob's descendants became the slaves of the Egyptians. The prospects of land faded and the hope for liberation replaced any illusion of land ownership.

As these Hebrews continue to increase, as related at the beginning of the book of Exodus, the Pharaoh of Egypt fears their growing population. "Look, the Israelite people are more numerous and powerful than we" (1:9). However, not only does he fear their growing number; he also worries that they will escape. Cheap labor—or slavery in this case—is a mainstay in maintaining a monarchy. Hence three times Pharaoh acts to curtail their ranks.

First he commands his officials to increase their burdens. Surely this will wear them down and diminish their strength. He sets taskmasters over them to "oppress them with forced labor" (1:11). While the detail of such treatment is often left untold, the description is briefly touched upon here. "The Egyptians became ruthless . . . made their lives bitter with hard service in mortar and brick and in every kind of field labor" (1:14). But God's promises to Israel could not be overshadowed or curtailed by even this powerful king and his malicious schemes. "But the more they were oppressed, the more they multiplied and spread" (1:12).

So in a second attempt to arrest the Israelites' growth the king designs a more murderous plan. He orders the two midwives of the Hebrews, Shiphrah and Puah, to kill the boys being born to the Israelites. Although we have little information about these women it is clear that the king had confidence in them. He enlisted these women to do his bidding. They are to be the instruments of the king's violence that he can hide behind. These agents of life have been ordered to abandon their social roles and become agents of death. However, the storyteller alerts us that the midwives "feared God" (1:17). As indicated by their actions, their reverence for God far exceeds their respect for the king. They refuse to act violently toward the women giving birth. They disobey Pharaoh and "did not do as the king of Egypt commanded them" (1:16). They let the boys live.

In contrast to the story of our cannibal mothers and the other biblical accounts of women set at odds with one another, these two midwives appear free enough to resist participating in a network of hostility and violence. Later we will consider why this is so. For now we note that Shiphrah and Puah decide against the king and in favor of the women and children. They choose to work with the other women in the interest of life. They refuse to violate the birthing women and their offspring in support of this monarch's scheme. In refusing to cooperate with this ruthless oppression they curtail the violence of its reign. God rewarded the midwives for their bravery and "gave them families" (1:21).

Two times now the Pharaoh's attempt to quell the swell in numbers among the Hebrews has failed. But this monarch will not be stopped. In a third attempt to cut off the increasing number of these Hebrews he issues a death order to be carried out by all his people. His murderous plan is comprehensive. "Every boy that is born to the Hebrews you shall throw into the Nile, but you shall let every girl live" (1:21).

Pharaoh's order has prompted the comment of many scholars. Some have noted how this despot's scheme is consistent with ancient practices. Unwanted children were often disposed of by exposure at a body of water. Hence the Pharaoh's order may not attract much attention or condemnation. On the other hand, some have commented on the absurdity of such a scheme. Curbing population in the ancient world was accomplished by destroying female children, not males. Therefore an order to kill all the boy babies could also indicate what a poor excuse he was for a king.[3]

However, the Pharaoh's death sentence for baby boys may be an indication of some other condition. Powerful sovereigns are desperate to insure control over the subjugated people on whom their reign and its extravagance depends. Given the impositions of harsh labor on the Hebrews, the Pharaoh had reason to fear a revolt on the part of those who bore arms or went to war. Typically in a patriarchal society these were men. Hence a difficult decision weighed upon this Pharaoh. Should he diminish the pool of manual laborers and deplete the work force for the years to come? This could threaten the integrity and sovereignty of the Egyptian kingdom. Or might he risk increasing that human resource and in the process chance a revolt? Since the nation states of the ancient world were frequently bolstered by slave laborers, the calamity of revolts was also well known. That Pharaoh orders the boy babies destroyed suggests the gravity of his fear. Any uprising would threaten the domestic well-being of a nation, but an uprising among the growing numbers of heavily burdened Hebrew slaves could jeopardize the security of the Pharaoh's powerful reign. Hence his decision to have the boy babies destroyed reinforces his expression of concern at the opening of the tale. He worries that because of the Hebrews' rapid and unchecked increase they will "in the event of war, join our enemies and fight against us and escape" (1:10).

---

[3] In "Depatriarchalizing in Biblical Interpretation," *Journal of the American Academy of Religion* 41 (1973) 34, Phyllis Trible commented that had Pharaoh anticipated the success of the women in foiling his orders and undercutting his murderous scheme he might have been wiser to order all the female infants killed.

When Part 2 opens, the lens on our story's camera narrows. It focuses on one of the Hebrew households affected by these difficult straits. We watch one Hebrew woman's response to this powerful monarch's threat to the life of her newborn son. First, consistent with the maternal instinct of a new mother, she hides her baby. But Pharaoh has issued his order to all his people. Living under such a comprehensive threat, she evidently comes to her senses about how long she can successfully conceal her child. Finally, after three months she admits to herself that "she could hide him no longer" (2:3). What initially sounds like resignation on the part of a slave woman before a powerful ruling tyrant makes sense. But this mother's resignation does not yield submission to the despot's ways. Instead, she designs and sets in motion a new plan to save her infant son. She fetches a basket for him that she secures with tar and pitch to waterproof what is to become his little ark. She sets him in it and places the basket among the reeds on the bank of the river. Exactly what she intends for him by this action is unclear. However, that she so carefully seals the basket so that no water can enter and threaten his well-being suggests she intends for him to live. She refuses to surrender his destiny and instead does what she can do to protect him. In doing so this powerless woman makes a decision to disobey the all-powerful Pharaoh. Tension is introduced into the story by her act of resistance. The baby's fate remains a question. The baby's sister is stationed at a distance where she can keep watch and "see what would happen to him" (2:4).

Tension is increased in the story when Pharaoh's daughter comes down to bathe at the river's edge. She and her maidservants are walking alongside the water when she spots the basket among the rushes. Upon her request one of her maidservants fetches the basket. When the Egyptian princess opens the basket she sees the crying baby and her heart is moved. Although she knows that "this must be one of the Hebrews' children," still "she took pity on him" (2:6). Positioned at some distance, the baby's sister evidently recognizes signs of the woman's care and concern for the child. Without explanation for her sudden presence before the princess and without permission to speak, the young girl seizes on the ripeness of the moment. She offers to find a woman from among the Hebrews to nurse the infant. When Pharaoh's daughter agrees, the girl goes and returns with the baby's mother.

The exchange between the Egyptian princess and the Hebrew mother is brief and businesslike. Pharaoh's daughter commissions her to "take this child and nurse it" (2:9). She also agrees to pay the Hebrew woman. Though we have only a description of their abbreviated exchange, we might wonder if something else is communicated silently and knowingly between these two women, something of which they dare not speak. According to their agreement, the child's mother then brings the boy to the daughter of Pharaoh after he is weaned. The Egyptian princess, who knew he was a Hebrew child, raises him as her own son. She calls him "Moses," a name derived from the Hebrew word *Moshe,* meaning "to draw out."

Despite the persistent threat to the increase of the Hebrews in Egypt, the first part of God's promise to the ancestors —"descendants as numerous as the stars"—continues in its fulfillment. Even in the most precarious of circumstances the Israelites increase. Now Moses, one of these descendants, will become God's instrument in realizing the second half of God's pledge of land expressed in Exodus. " And I will give you a land, a land flowing with milk and honey" (cf. 3:8).

## Overturning Textual Violence

When we read this story in Exodus in conjunction with the other stories we have considered, this tale of two mothers—a birth mother and an adoptive mother—becomes a counter text. Parallels in the story line link it both with our tale of the cannibal mothers and with the other pairs of women characters we considered. We are drawn to read them together. Once again the issue of life, born or unborn, is at the heart of the crises among women. The matter of power, both monarchial and patriarchal, provokes and fuels the crises. The consequences of these forces, a classist society, stand ready to breed and nurture violence.

Like the tale of the cannibal mothers, the story in Exodus is told in the interest of those with power. In the case of the cannibal mothers the machinations of the king and prophet constitute the nucleus of the story. In the instance of the Exodus tale the birth of Moses and his eventual rivalry with the Pharaoh are considered center stage. Like the cannibal mothers, most of the women characters in the Exodus story have no names. However, in their namelessness they are less anonymous than the cannibal mothers. As with Rachel, Leah, Sarah, and Hagar we know them by virtue of the men they stand in relation to. The princess is Pharaoh's daughter and the women accompanying her to the water are maidservants of his house. The woman who gives birth to the child is the wife of a man from the house of Levi. Later she receives further specification as Moses' mother. Finally, the girl watching over the infant at the water's edge and then later negotiating the care of the infant with the Pharaoh's daughter is known to us as Moses' sister. Here the patriarchal base of fathers and husbands by which nameless women receive identification expands to include even infant sons. Moses' mother and sister are identified with reference to this infant. In patriarchal society even an endangered baby crying in a basket floating among the reeds on the bank of a river is less anonymous than the women who save him. Moreover, he becomes the point of reference by which women in this tale have identity and importance in the story—not only Moses' mother and his sister, but also the maidservants who fetch him and the princess who raises him as her own son.

It is extremely curious and, as we will see, more than just interesting that two of the female characters in the wider story do have names. The midwives to the Hebrews, two seemingly adjunct characters to the controversy that provokes the central tension in the tale—the threat posed by the increasing number of Israelites to the Pharaoh followed by the rivalry between Moses and Pharaoh later in the book—are introduced by name, Shiphrah and Puah. They are not identified as being from their fathers' house, nor are they referenced as wives of any man. In fact, they are named before even the baby, Moses, is introduced into the account. Moreover, while Pharaoh enlists their service it is not clear that they are members of Pharaoh's royal forces or employees.

A question surrounding translation of the text here further cloaks their exact identities. If we render the text "midwives of the Hebrews" the two women might well be Egyptian. In this regard some have argued that Shiphrah is an Egyptian name. However, the text can also be translated "Hebrew midwives," which argues for their Hebrew identity. Hence the text itself invites uncertainty about their ethnicity. That the Pharaoh summons these women to be his instruments of violence argues in favor of their Egyptian nationality. However, it is also possible to argue that it is an unlikely scenario to have Egyptian women offering such intimate service to women who were considered slaves in that society. Though the debate continues, it remains inconclusive as to whether they are Hebrew or Egyptian. Hence we cannot say for certain who they are by virtue of national allegiance. Thus with these women not identified by household, lacking all ties to fathers, husbands, or sons, and in the absence of clear political or national affiliation, we don't know who they are. Yet they are named. The irregularity of these conditions in the biblical traditions thus far is certainly of note. Moreover, they are the only characters in this cast to be named until the Pharaoh's daughter utters Moses' name at the end of the story.

Though we do not know anything about the women's connections, or who they are related to, the narrative does give us some information about them. Their brief description as "midwives" tells us something about who they are by virtue of what they do. We know that as midwives they worked within the private and exclusive sphere of women giving birth. In this ancient context such women were the emissaries of life. Such responsibility required single-minded devotion to the immediacy and precariousness of their task. Utmost attention and fidelity were required in the miraculous as well as dangerous activity in which they participated. Midwives were the liaisons between the womb and the world. How seriously did they take their responsibility? Not even a king's order for murder and the probable consequences of disobedience to such a command could dissuade these midwives from their vocation. To do otherwise would be to betray their identity and undercut their self-understanding. Moreover, to abandon their responsibilities would jeopardize more than the midwives' standing; midwives' infidelity to their role among the people would put the whole community at risk.

However, the midwives' decision to disobey Pharaoh not only bespeaks a kind of steadfastness characteristic of their very profession; the story indicates a further motive. The midwives "feared God" (1:17). In the Hebrew tradition fear of the LORD was not indicative of worry and anxiety, but of reverence. It indicates a knowledge that beholds and stands in awe of the utter mystery of the divine. Fear suggests a healthy reverence before this marvelous Unknown. When they are confronted with the choice between obeying the Pharaoh they can see and the God they cannot see, their decision witnesses their great faith. They believe in the God of life; hence they disobey the Pharaoh and protect the infants. Moreover, their resistance to this monarchal authority initiates a new direction for the Exodus story. The violence and oppression of this Pharaoh are about to be curtailed. This story of oppression and subjugation is on the brink of becoming a tale of liberation. The midwives not only deliver babies; they also set in motion the deliverance of this enslaved people. Not only does the fate of Moses rest on their courageous decision; the future of the whole Hebrew people depends on their rejection of Pharaoh's murderous scheme.

While we do not know who they are, that Shiphrah and Puah are named guarantees that they are remembered for their great deeds. Their resistance acts as antidote to the kind of violence we have witnessed across other biblical narratives. Outside the bonds of patriarchy and opposed to the warrants of monarchy, two women refuse to act against other women. By this one deed they change the course of the story and counter the oppression of the king. Moreover, their counter-action is as far-reaching as the violence it curtails. Once begun, a decision to stem violence cannot be checked. Its course is as infectious as the violence it opposes. Hence their life-preserving action leads to another woman's decision to resist this deadly despot.

Moses' mother also refuses submission to the tyrant's deadly order. When she realizes she can no longer hide her infant son, she resists despair.

While the king orders that all boy babies perish in the Nile, she counters his order with her deed. She preserves her son on the Nile. Instead of waiting for him to be discovered and then cast into the river, she acts to save him. She places him in a basket that she sets on the water's edge. We do not know specifically what she intended by this action, but her plan for the child is clear. She wills him to live in the face of an order for death. Moreover, though powerless, she is willing to risk the consequences for a slave woman who defies the order of the all-powerful monarch. We can only imagine with horror what such punishment might entail.

What prompted this act of courage? Was the basket placed among the reeds in order to camouflage it? Or did she hope it would be discovered? Did the woman know that Pharaoh's daughter and her maidservants would be walking along the water? Or did the deeds of the midwives inspire her to act in the interest of life? Perhaps she, too, feared God and understood a greater truth—that the preservation of life itself would make demands on her personally. She would have to surrender her son.

As we noted earlier, such courage not only counters violence but, like the violence it opposes, this courage cannot be easily curtailed. As our story continues this commitment to act in the interest of life spreads and now finds companionship in a daughter. Moses' sister is positioned at a distance to watch the bobbing bassinet at the river's edge. Even this young girl demonstrates her capacity for resistance. While the narrator's description attempts to contain her, her character refuses to remain "watching at a distance." When the Pharaoh's daughter and her maidservants discover the child, Moses' sister seizes the moment. Without explanation for her sudden appearance or apology for addressing a member of the royal household, she speaks to the Egyptian princess. Moses' sister acts on her intuitions. She evidently sensed and interpreted the sentiments of compassion that Pharaoh's daughter feels for the child. The young girl also anticipates the potential problem that might compromise these feelings and proposes a solution. The baby needs to be nursed and she knows someone among the Hebrew women who can help. With no lack of gumption, and with an excess of straightforwardness, she says, "Shall I go and get you a nurse from the Hebrew women to nurse the child for you?" (2:7). Her question hints at this young girl's expectation of this adult to care for the child. This is a subtle but remarkable challenge to the reigning ethos of relations in both patriarchal and monarchal society. Here the young powerless one sets forth expectations of the older powerful one to which the Egyptian responds. She urges the infant's sister, "Yes, go!" (2:8).

In addition, the Egyptian princess has acknowledged in the presence of her maidservants that the infant was a Hebrew boy. Hence the web of women cooperating in the interest of life has expanded even further here. The commitment to life that was acted out between two midwives and the Hebrew women they attended has now extended to this member of Pharaoh's own family. Away from the palace and in the presence of other women she is unconstrained; she can feel compassion even for a Hebrew child and act on those feelings. Her decision to preserve the child is a remarkable act of bravery. A family member who acts against the monarch's orders risks more than disobeying the law. She chances chastisement of the royal household and making a mockery of the king. Would there not be consequences for even Pharaoh's own daughter if she publicly shamed her father? And were not the maidservants also risking being held in contempt of the ruler's plan? Certainly they could be convenient targets for blame in order to shift the guilt from the Pharaoh's daughter and save face.

When Moses' mother comes before the Egyptian princess the dynamic of relations that undercuts the violence becomes widespread and explicit. First the Egyptian princess orders Moses' mother to take the child and suckle him. This follows the typical pattern of one with power issuing commands to the powerless. However, Pharaoh's daughter follows her command with a promise of payment for these services. What starts out as an exchange mirroring the social inequalities between these two women becomes a just agreement. The child's birth mother will suckle the child; the adoptive mother will pay her; and in keeping with their agreement Moses' mother brings him to the Egyptian woman when the child is weaned. The Hebrew woman gave birth to the child and the Egyptian woman raises him as her son.

## Conclusion

In contrast to all the other stories of women at odds with one another over the life of a child, in this account in Exodus women are working together to preserve an infant's life. When we considered the story of the cannibal mothers, the two harlots before a king, the story of Sarah and Hagar, and the account of Rachel and Leah, we were surrounded with women who were encumbered by a network of oppression and violence. Women at odds with one another appeared as referential context for telling men's stories or even for saying something great about kings, prophets, or patriarchs. Hence dynamics of patriarchy and hegemony, where the powerful were also the privileged or main characters, coincided with stories of women, often as minor characters who were at odds with one another over the matter of life.

The violence and oppression surrounding the characters of the cannibal mothers cannot be denied or ignored. Nor should it be excised from a canon that claims to be a religious text. Like the Inquisition, the Holocaust, or the numerous other tragedies in human history, the regular recitation and recall of such events and their victims etches in the forefront of our consciousness the atrocities of which we are capable as humans. Though their characters may be minor (like the woman in the restaurant at the beginning of our book), they teach us lessons about privilege, power, violence, and the value of life in our journey to build our own character.

For all the horror and travesty of these tales, they do not have the last word. Stories like the Exodus account act as counter texts and disclose what can happen when people work together. In this network of cooperation the characteristic dividing lines of ethnicity, social class, and age that order a classist society are traversed. Inspired perhaps by Shiphrah and Puah, who appear to stand outside the encumbrances of both patriarchy and monarchy, a mother and daughter work together. A woman of the royal class cooperates with a woman from the servant class. Maidservants are made accomplices with the plan of a princess. An adult woman goes along with a young child's proposal. The political and ethnic differences of Egyptian and Hebrew are transgressed. All the lines that divide and segregate persons from one another—lines of class, age, ethnicity, power, social standing—are here transgressed. In the process, the network of divisions and violence at the heart of patriarchy and hegemony is abandoned. As a result of this affront to the violence of patriarchy and hegemony life is not only preserved; life is fostered in such a way that an entire people is eventually liberated.

The characters of our cannibal mothers have not only taken us on a journey through other stories but have exposed our own capacity for harm and violence toward one another. As we have noted, the ways we read and interpret texts can be acts of violence or acts of resistance. And how we read is not unrelated to how we live. At the same time our study of the cannibal mothers' characters invites us to consider counter stories, not only those in texts like Exod 1:8–2:10 but also counter stories we have witnessed in others' courageous choices and the counter stories we might write with our own lives.

Throughout history, hostilities, wars, famines, and threats of annihilation are among the myriad forms of violence exchanged by those jockeying for sovereignty or power and visited upon those subjugated by these antics. The maintenance of such atrocities depends upon polarization of peoples and the cultivation of violence among those who might collectively protest. People willing to acknowledge their differences, willing to work across lines that divide them, willing to resist polarization among themselves—whether in Kabul, Hebron, New York City, or even in the

Church—create an affront to this chain of violence. Such determination to work together composes a contemporary counter text, insuring that the violence narrated in the biblical tales and the societal violence too often reinforced by a heritage of such texts and their interpretation will not have the last word.

# BIBLIOGRAPHY

Adam, A.K.M., ed. *Handbook of Postmodern Biblical Interpretation.* 2 vols. St. Louis: Chalice, 2000.

_____. *What Is Postmodern Biblical Criticism?* Minneapolis: Fortress, 1995.

Alter, Robert. *The Art of Biblical Narrative.* New York: Basic Books, 1981.

Ashcroft, Bill, Gareth Griffiths, and Helen Tiffin, eds. *The Post-Colonial Studies Reader.* London and New York: Routledge, 1995.

Bach, Alice. "Signs of the Flesh: Observations on Characterization in the Bible," *Semeia* 63 (1993) 61–79.

Bailie, Gil. *Violence Unveiled: Humanity at the Crossroads.* New York: Crossroad, 1995.

Bar Efrat, Shimon. *Narrative Art in the Bible.* Sheffield: Almond Press, 1989.

Berlin, Adele. *Poetics and Interpretation of Biblical Narrative.* Winona Lake: Eisenbrauns, 1994.

Bible and Culture Collective. *The Postmodern Bible.* New Haven: Yale University Press, 1995.

Bird, Phyllis. "The Harlot as Heroine: Narrative Art and Social Presupposition in Three Old Testament Texts," *Semeia* 46 (1989) 32.

Brueggemann, Walter. *1 & 2 Kings.* Smyth and Helwys Bible Commentary. Macon, Ga.: Smyth and Helwys, 2000.

_____, and Hans Walter Wolff. *The Vitality of the Old Testament Traditions.* Atlanta: John Knox, 1982.

Camp, Claudia. "1 and 2 Kings," in Carol A. Newsom and Sharon H. Ringe, eds., *The Women's Bible Commentary.* London: S.P.C.K.; Louisville: Westminster John Knox, 1992.

Chatman, Seymour. *Story and Discourse.* Ithaca: Cornell University Press, 1978.

Cogan, Mordechai, and Hayim Tadmor. *II Kings.* Anchor Bible Commentary 11. Garden City, N.Y.: Doubleday, 1988.

Coote, Robert, ed. *Elijah and Elisha in Socioliterary Perspective.* Atlanta: Scholars, 1992.

Exum, J. Cheryl. *Plotted, Shot, and Painted: Cultural Representations of Biblical Women.* Sheffield: Sheffield Academic Press, 1996.

_____. "'You Shall Let Every Daughter Live': A Study of Exodus 1:8–2:10," *Semeia* 28 (1983) 63–82.

Fretheim, Terence E. *Deuteronomic History.* Interpreting Biblical Texts. Nashville: Abingdon, 1983.

Gray, John. *I & II Kings. A Commentary.* 2nd ed. Philadelphia: Westminster, 1970.

Hens-Piazza, Gina. "Forms of Violence and the Violence of Forms—Two Cannibal Mothers Before a King (2 Kings 6:24-33)," *Journal of Feminist Studies in Religion* 14 (1998) 91–104.

_____. "Violence in Joshua and Judges," *The Bible Today* 39 (July 2001) 196–203.

Hochman, Baruch. *Character in Literature.* Ithaca: Cornell University Press, 1985.

Jones, Gwilym. *1 and 2 Kings.* New Century Bible Commentary 2. Grand Rapids: Eerdmans, 1984.

LaBarbera, Robert. "The Man of War and the Man of God: Social Satire in 2 Kings 6:8–7:20," *CBQ* 46 (1984) 646.

Lasine, Stuart, and Hugh Pyper. "Judging the Wisdom of Solomon: The Two-Way Effect of Intertextuality," *Journal for the Study of the Old Testament* 59 (1993) 25–36.

Lasine, Stuart. "Jehoram and the Cannibal Mothers (2 Kings 6:24-33): Solomon's Judgment in an Inverted World," *Journal for the Study of the Old Testament* 50 (1991) 27–53.

_____. "The Ups and Downs of Monarchical Justice: Solomon and Jehoram in an Intertextual World," *Journal for the Study of the Old Testament* 59 (1993) 37–53.

Muilenburg, James. "Form Criticism and Beyond," *Journal of Biblical Literature* 88 (1969) 1–18.

Nelson, Richard. *First and Second Kings.* Interpretation. Louisville: John Knox, 1987.

Provan, Iain. *1 and 2 Kings.* New International Biblical Commentary. Peabody, Mass.: Hendrickson, 1995.

Robinson, Joseph. *The Second Book of Kings.* London, New York, and Melbourne: Cambridge University Press, 1976.

Trible, Phyllis. *God and the Rhetoric of Sexuality.* Philadelphia: Fortress, 1978.

Wenham, Gordon. *Genesis 16–50.* Word Biblical Commentary 2. Eds. David A. Hubbard and Glen Barker. Waco: Word Books, 1994.

Wiseman, Donald. *1 and 2 Kings.* Leicester: InterVarsity Press, 1993.